Microwave Cookbook
SAMSUNG

To Our Valued Customer:

Welcome to the most versatile system of food preparation ever devised by man.
You are about to embark on an entirely new way of life that you will find more
convenient and pleasurable.
Suddenly, you will discover lower power bills, more leisure time and delicious, nutritious
food never before possible without great effort and toil.
We at Samsung like to believe that we are instrumental in providing you with a better
quality of life through out technology and consumer products.
This cookbook is your "roadmap" to that better life. Please read the introduction
carefully and proceed to enjoy the numerous time-tested recipes offered.
After you are experienced in microwave cooking, you will be able to devise new uses
and new recipes for your microwave oven.
We cordially invite you to share your experiences and ideas with us. We are pleased
that you bought a Samsung appliance and we look forward to serving you in the future.

-sincerely-

HOME APPLIANCE DIVISION
TEST KITCHEN
SAMSUNG ELECTRONICS CO., LTD.
416 MAETAN-DONG, SUWOEN,
KYUNGKI DO, KOREA

MAIL ADDRESS:
Samsung Electronics America Inc.
117 Serview Drive
Secaucus, NJ 07094 U.S.A.

Contents

THE THEORY OF MICROWAVE COOKING

Microwaves are short, high frequency radio waves similar to those you receive on a TV set. They are generated by an electronic tube called a magnetron. From the magnetron tube, microwaves enter through openings located in the top of the oven, penetrate and heat the food in the oven. In order to obtain uniform heat distribution in the food, the microwaves are evenly distributed by a device called a "stirrer". The stirrer, shaped like a fan, scatters the microwaves evenly throughout the oven.

Microwaves have three characteristics. Microwave energy can be:

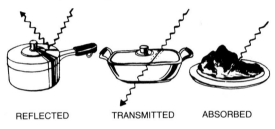

REFLECTED   TRANSMITTED   ABSORBED

REFLECTION

Microwaves are reflected by metal objects, therefore, the oven interior is coated with epoxy paint for reflection purposes. A mechanical stirrer distributes the microwaves evenly throughout the oven.

TRANSMISSION

Microwaves will pass harmlessly through materials such as glass, ceramics, paper and certain plastics. No change takes place in these materials since they do not absorb or reflect microwaves. This is why cooking utensils made of these materials are ideal for cooking and remain cool in a microwave oven. The heat that can build up in these utensils is from the food, not the microwaves.

ABSORPTION

Anything that is moist will absorb microwaves. When microwaves enter moist objects, a molecular reaction occurs. The molecules begin to vibrate causing heat by friction. This action causes the food to cook.

Microwaves can penetrate food up to a depth of one inch.

Large foods are cooked internally by conduction of the vibrating molecules toward the center. Microwaves dissipate and cannot be retained in food.

MICROWAVE COOKING UTENSILS

Microwave cooking offers a host of conveniences in selection of cooking utensils. New shapes and materials are developed and introduced all the time. Don't, however, run out and buy all new cooking utensils. First, inventory the cooking utensils you already have on hand. You will be surprised at how many items you already have that are microwave oven safe.

GLASS-CERAMIC-CHINAWARE are excellent for use in a microwave oven provided they do not have metal parts or metallic trim on them. Most fine chinaware is decorated or trimmed in gold, platinum or silver and is very thin or delicate and should not be used in a microwave oven. The thicker, sturdier chinaware, without trim, however, is suitable. Delicate glassware should not be used as it cannot stand the stress of heat and may break. The heat is transmitted from the contents to the utensil, which causes breakage.

Ceramic mugs or cups with glued on handles should not be used as the glue will absorb microwaves and separation will occur. Dishware that is cracked or crazed should not be used as they may not be able to withstand heat.

Several manufacturers identify microwave oven safe utensils either on the utensil itself or with an accompanying brochure.

One of the most popular manufacturers of microwave utensils is Corning®. Corning® now marks its products "good for microwave" or "good for range and microwave." Corning's Pyrex® without metallic trim is also microwave oven safe.

Centura tableware and Corelle® closed handle cups (both by Corning) cannot be used in the microwave oven.

Other popular manufacturers of microwave oven safe utensils are Fire King® by Anchor Hocking, French Cookware® by Marsh Industries, Glassbake® by Jeannette Glass,

Glass Ovenware® by Heller Designs and products by Federal Glass®. Dinnerware such as Temper-Ware® by Lenox and Franciscan® Casual China that is marked ovenproof is usually safe to use. The following heat-resistant glass cookware is highly recommended for microwave use:

- Loaf dishes
- Mixing bowls
- Measuring cups
- Round or square cake dishes
- Casserole dishes, (3-qt. maximum)
- Oblong baking dishes (10 x 6 x 2-inch maximum)
- Custard cups

With all the varieties available remember a few simple basic rules:

DO NOT USE:
- Utensils with metal bands, clips, screws or trim
- Delicate glassware or stemware
- Dishware that is cracked or crazed
- Mugs or cups with glued handles

WHEN IN DOUBT:
How to test a utensil for safe microwave oven use:
- Measure 1 cup of water in a glass cup.
- Place in the oven on or beside the utensil to be tested.
- Heat for 3 minutes at HIGH POWER. If the utensil is warm, it has absorbed some microwave energy and should not be used. If the container is microwave oven safe, it should remain cool and the water should be hot.

PAPER is a convenient product to use for food with low moisture or fat content. The cooking time should be short in duration. Napkins, paper towels, cups, plates, cardboard, freezer wrap and wax paper are all handy utensils. Avoid wax-coated plates and cups as the heavy coating of wax will melt due to high food temperatures. Wax paper, however, can be used to prevent food spatters. Paper is also used to absorb fat and excess moisture. For example, a popular way to cook bacon is to place a paper towel or napkin on a paper plate. Lay bacon strips side by side on the towel or napkin and cover with another napkin or towel. The paper will absorb the excess bacon grease.

CAUTION: Some recycled paper products may contain impurities that could cause arcing or may ignite.

JARS AND BOTTLES: Avoid heating baby food in jars. Remove metal caps to warm syrup or soften salad dressing from refrigerator.
Jars which are not heat tempered should not be used to heat food.
Most vegetables and entrees are best removed to glass or plastic microwave safe container.

PLASTIC: Dishes, cups and some freezer containers can be used in the microwave oven.
Choose carefully, however, because thin items may melt or become pitted from the heat of the food. A "dishwasher safe" label is a good sign that the container will also be microwave oven safe. Plastic should not be used for cooking over an extended period of time or with foods having a high fat or sugar content.
- Containers labeled UDEL® (by Union Carbide) and polysulfone plastic are very durable for microwave cooking.

PLASTIC WRAP may be used in place of lids to cover dishes for most recipes. It is advisable to turn back one corner about 1 inch to allow excessive steam to escape. Remove plastic wrap slowly and away from you to avoid steam burns.

COOKING BAGS designed for conventional oven use may be used in a microwave oven provided small slits are made near the top of the bag to allow excess steam to escape. Do not use wire twist ties.

CAUTION: Do not use ordinary plastic storage bags for cooking.

HEAVY STRAW, WICKER AND WOOD UTENSILS may be used in your microwave oven for short periods in order to warm bread and rolls. Large or thick wooden utensils should not be used for prolonged periods as they may become very dry and brittle.

METAL UTENSILS must be avoided in microwave cooking. Utensils with metal straps, fasteners, clips or screws should not be used as they may cause arcing. Arcing may cause damage to the oven walls. ALUMINUM FOIL may be used in small strips to cover the wings of chickens, tips of roasts or other thin parts of meat that tend to overcook. The foil will slow the cooking of these areas since metal reflects microwaves. This will prevent overcooking.

Using foil on Roast

Using foil when cooking chicken.

FOIL LINED CONTAINERS should NOT be used in a microwave oven. Metal trays may be used for T.V. Dinners. They should be no higher than ¾-inch for best results. Remove foil cover. Keep metal at least one inch from sides of microwave oven.

TWIST TIES should be removed. They may cause bag to heat and may cause fire.

METAL SKEWERS may be used if the food mass is large in proportion to the metal. Exercise care in placing the skewers in the oven to prevent arcing between skewers or between the sides of the oven and the skewers. Wooden skewers are preferred and can be purchased in most grocery and department stores.

THERMOMETERS for use in microwave cooking are specially designed for that purpose and available in most department stores.

CAUTION: Do not use conventional mercury, candy or meat thermometers in your microwave oven.

BROWNING DISHES are used to sear various cuts of meat and meat patties. The dish must first be preheated several minutes at HIGH POWER. This will allow the special coating on the bottom of the dish to absorb microwave energy and become very hot.

When foods are placed in the browning dish, searing will occur. The following suggestions are offered for proper care and use of browning dishes:

- Preheat dish according to accompanying directions.
- Check information included with browning dish before use.
- Add oil or butter only after preheating.
- Use pot holders or oven glove to remove dish from oven.
- Never use browning dishes on gas or electric ranges or in conventional ovens.
- Do not use browning dish and temperature probe together.
- Clean in dishwasher or with hot, sudsy water. Do not use steel wool, plastic scrubbing pads or scouring powder on surface of browning dish.

OTHER BROWNING TECHNIQUES: Meats and poultry cooked 10 to 15 minutes brown from their own juices. Foods cooked for shorter periods can be aided with the help of browning sauces such as Worcestershire sauce or soy sauce, brushed over the meat before heating. These sauces neither add nor take away from the original flavor of the meat. Baked goods will not brown but a number of toppings may be used to enhance the appearance.

SPECIAL HINTS FOR PREPARING RECIPES

Ingredients

All ingredients are used as taken from their normal storage area. As an example, eggs and milk would be added to the recipe cold since they would be taken from the refrigerator. Canned ingredients should include the liquid unless the recipe specifies DRAINED. Other recipe factors are:

- Flour—use all-purpose.
- Milk—use homogenized whole milk.
- Sugar—use granulated white sugar.
- Eggs—use grade A large.
- Amounts—use cup, teaspoon, etc. for standard measure.

Factors Which Affect Cooking

Several factors which influence timing and results in conventional cooking are exaggerated by microwave speed.

Timing

A cooking time range (example: 2½ to 3 minutes) is given in each recipe. The reasons are to allow for varied food shapes and electrical volt output which is changeable during peak usage hours. Remember, time can always be added to properly cook various recipes. Once food is overcooked, however, the situation cannot be reversed. An APPROXIMATE COOKING TIME is given for each recipe. If a recipe is cooked in two batches, the approximate cooking time includes extra cooking time.

Spacing

When possible, arrange smaller food items in a circular pattern for equal microwave energy distribution. This applies to potatoes, fruit or hors d'oeuvres. When placing food in baking dish, always place around the edges. Never stack foods on top of each other.

Arrange food in circular pattern.

Turning & Rotating

Repositioning a dish in the oven helps food cook evenly. To rotate ½ turn, turn the dish until the side which was to the back of the oven is to the front.
To rotate ¼ turn, turn the dish until the side which was to the back of the oven is to the side.
When microwaving, turning is often needed during defrosting, or when cooking foods such as hamburgers from the frozen state.

Stirring

When stirring is necessary, it is best to bring the cooked outside edges toward the center and the less cooked center toward the edges. Recipes will indicate the amount of stirring required.

Covering

Covering foods reduces spattering and shortens cooking times by retaining heat. One's choice of cover also helps control the rate of evaporation in a particular recipe. For example, if you want to develop a drier surface, don't cover or use a paper towel. For maximum moisture retention, use a glass lid or plastic wrap. Remember, all covers must allow for a certain amount of pressure to be released. In using plastic wrap, be sure to make a small slit in the top to allow excess steam to escape.

Standing Time

Most foods continue cooking by conduction after removing from the oven. Standing time is necessary for the center portions of food to complete cooking without overcooking the outside. Meats should stand 10 to 15 minutes while a shorter time is required for casseroles and vegetables.

Converting Recipes from Conventional Cooking to Microwave Cooking

If you want to use an old favorite recipe in your new microwave oven, timing is probably the most difficult factor to consider. A few basic rules are suggested:

- Reduce conventional cooking time to ¼ for microwave use.
- Try to find a similar recipe and use the same time and temperature.
- Do not add salt to meat before cooking as it tends to toughen meat. Other spices may be used freely. Salt may be added after cooking.
- In baked goods, reduce leavening agents by ¼ and increase liquids by ¼. Baking hints are offered on pages 76 and 82.
- Ingredients for stews and casseroles should be sliced to a uniform size for even cooking.

INFORMATION FOR REHEATING FOODS.

When all members of the family cannot eat at one time, reheating is a great benefit.
You can reheat a combination of precooked foods on one plate.
Remember, reheated foods need only be heated to a temperature comfortable to the palate.
Some general guidelines to follow:

- Place only one plate at a time inside the oven.
- Cover dish with either a lid or plastic wrap to retain moisuture. The food will heat faster.
- Arrange thick areas and dense foods to the outside of dish, with easy-to-heat foods on the inside.

PRECAUTIONS TO AVOID POSSIBLE EXPOSURE TO EXCESSIVE MICROWAVE ENERGY

(a) Do not attempt to operate this oven with the door open since open-door operation can result in harmful exposure to microwave energy. It is important not to defeat or tamper with the safety interlocks.

(b) Do not place any object between the oven front face and the door or allow soil or cleaner residue to accumulate on sealing surfaces.

(c) Do not operate the oven if it is damaged. It is particularly important that the oven door close properly and that there is no damage to the:
      (1) door (bent)
      (2) hinges and latches (broken or loosened)
      (3) door seals and sealing surfaces

(d) The oven should not be adjusted or repaired by anyone except properly qualified service personnel.

COOKING PRECAUTIONS FOR MICROWAVE OVEN

(a) Eggs must not be cooked or reheated in the shell, or with an unbroken yolk.
Pierce the yolk with a fork or knife before cooking.
(b) Pierce the "skin" of potatoes, whole squash, apples, sausages, chicken livers and other giblets to prevent bursting.
(c) Deep fat frying can not be done in the microwave oven.
(d) Do not operate the oven while empty. Food or liquid should be in the oven during operation to absorb microwave energy.
(e) Do not pop popcorn unless you use an accessory designed for this purpose.

Pictured on the following page: Hot Canapes. Meatball Tidbits▶

CRUNCHY MUNCHIES

Approx. Cooking Time: 12 min.
Yield: 24 hors d'oeuvres

1 head (about 1 1/2 lbs.) cauliflower*
**1 package (2 3/8 oz.) Italian flavored
seasoned coating mix**

1. Cut cauliflower into about 24 flowerets;
   rinse. Empty coating mix into plastic bag
   and coat cauliflowerets.
2. On glass plate, arrange 12 in circular
   pattern and heat 5 to 6 minutes until tender.
   Let stand 3 minutes before serving;
   repeat procedure.

*****Variation:** *Use 1 pound zucchini, cut
into 1/2-inch slices.*

CRANBERRY GLAZED FRANKFURTERS

Approx. Cooking Time: 14 min.
Yield: 36 hors d'oeuvres

**1 can (8 oz.) whole berry or jellied
cranberry sauce**
1 tablespoon lemon juice
1 1/2 tablespoons prepared mustard
1 pound cocktail frankfurters*

1. In square baking dish, combine cranberry
   sauce, lemon juice and mustard. Heat 4
   to 5 minutes, stirring once.
2. Stir frankfurters into glaze mixture. Heat
   8 to 9 minutes stirring once. To serve,
   skewer frankfurters with toothpicks.

*****Substitution:** *Use 1 pound frankfurters,
cut into 1 1/2-inch pieces
for cocktail frankfurters.*

COCKTAIL REUBENS

Approx. Cooking Time: 9 min.
Yield: 36 hors d'oeuvres

36 slices party-size rye bread
1/2 cup creamy Russian dressing
1/4 pound thinly sliced corned beef
1 can (8 oz.) sauerkraut, drained
**6 slices (rectangular) Swiss
cheese, each cut into 6 pieces**

1. Spread bread with dressing; top with
   corned beef, sauerkraut and cheese.
   Arrange 12 on plate or serving platter.
2. Heat 2 to 3 minutes until cheese is melted;
   repeat procedure.

CHILI DIP

Approx. Cooking Time: 12 min.
Yield: 2 cups

1/2 pound ground beef
1/2 cup finely chopped onion
1 can (6 oz.) tomato paste
**1 envelope (1 1/4 oz.) chili season-
ing mix**
1 tablespoon sugar (optional)

1. In medium glass bowl, crumble ground
   beef; stir in onions. Heat 5 to 6 minutes
   until beef is browned, stirring once; drain.
2. Stir in tomato paste, chili seasoning, and
   sugar. Heat 5 to 6 minutes.
3. Serve warm with corn chips.

CHICKEN TOTS

Approx. Cooking Time: 4 to 5 min.
Yield: 24 hors d'oeuvres

**2 cans (5 oz. ea.) boned chicken,
drained and flaked**
2 tablespoons parsley flakes
3 tablespoons mayonnaise
2 tablespoons dry bread crumbs
2 tablespoons dried onion flakes
1/4 teaspoon curry powder
1 egg, beaten
1/2 cup dry bread crumbs

1. Combine chicken, parsley, mayonnaise,
   2 tablespoons bread crumbs, onion, curry
   and egg. Shape into 24 balls. Roll each
   ball in bread crumbs; chill.
2. Arrange 12 balls on glass plate and heat
   4 to 5 minutes, giving plate 1/4 turn after 2
   minutes; repeat procedure. Serve, if
   desired, with curried mayonnaise or
   mustard sauce.

BACON TREATS

Approx. Cooking Time: 6 min.
Yield: 8 hors d'oeuvres

> **4 slices bacon, halved**
> **8 frozen potato puffs, canned pineapple chunks or water chestnuts**

1. Between layers of paper towel on paper plate, heat bacon 2½ to 3 minutes until partially cooked.
2. Wrap bacon around potato and secure with toothpick. Arrange on paper towel lined plate and heat 2 to 3 minutes.

CHEESE'N BACON STICKS

Approx. Cooking Time: 6 to 8 min.
Yield: 8 pieces

> **4 slices bacon**
> **8 pencil-thin cheese flavored bread sticks**

1. Cut bacon in half lengthwise, and wrap each half around bread stick in spiral fashion. Line a glass plate with 2 layers of paper towels.
2. Place the bread sticks on the plate and cover with a single paper towel. Heat for 6 to 8 minutes until crisp.

SWISS DELIGHTS

Approx. Cooking Time: 4 min.
Yield: 20 hors d'oeuvres

> **½ cup sour cream**
> **1 pkg. (½ oz.) instant onion soup Whole wheat crackers (about 20)**
> **2 slices (rectangular) Swiss cheese, each cut into 10 squares**

1. Blend sour cream and instant onion soup completely; spread mixture on each cracker and top with cheese.
2. Arrange 10 pieces in a circular pattern on a glass tray. Heat, uncovered, for 1 to 2 minutes until cheese melts giving plate ¼ turn once during cooking. Repeat for remaining crackers.

CRABMEAT SUPREME

Approx. Cooking Time: 1 min.
Yield: 8 canapes

> **½ can (3 to 3½ oz.) crabmeat**
> **¼ cup finely minced celery**
> **1 teaspoon prepared mustard**
> **2 teaspoons chopped sweet pickle relish**
> **¼ cup mayonnaise Crisp crackers or toast round**

1. Drain crabmeat and place in a small bowl. Flake with a fork. Add celery, mustard, pickle relish and mayonnaise. Blend well. Spread mixture on crackers or toast rounds.
2. Place on a glass plate lined with a paper towel. Cover and heat for ½ to 1 minute until hot.

HAM ROLL-UPS

Approx. Cooking Time: 12 min.
Yield: 40 hors d'oeuvres

> **1 pound cooked ham, thinly sliced**
> **2 tablespoons prepared brown mustard**
> **1 pound American cheese slices**

1. Spread each slice of ham with mustard. Place a slice of cheese on each slice of ham and roll from the short end so that the cheese is completely enclosed in the ham. Cut roll-ups in quarters crosswise and secure ends of ham with wooden toothpicks. Arrange 20 in a single layer on a glass plate.
2. Heat, uncovered, 5½ to 6 minutes until ham is hot and cheese is melted. Repeat for remaining roll-ups.

MEATBALL TIDBITS

Approx. Cooking Time: 7 min.
Yield: 36 meatballs

- **1 pound ground beef**
- **1 egg**
- **1/2 cup soft bread crumbs**
- **1/4 cup catsup**
- **1 tablespoon parsley flakes**
- **1 teaspoon onion powder**
- **1 teaspoon salt**
- **1/8 teaspoon pepper**

1. Thoroughly combine all ingredients; shape into 1-inch meatballs (about 36).
2. In oblong baking dish, arrange meatballs; heat 6 to 7 minutes, stirring once and draining liquid when necessary.
3. Serve with favorite sauce or gravy.

Hint: *See Sauces and Toppings chapter for easy microwave accompaniments.*

MARINATED VEGETABLE BITES

Approx. Cooking Time: 10 min.
Yield: 4 cups

- **4 cups cut-up fresh vegetables (about 1/2-in. pieces)***
- **1/2 cup Italian dressing**

1. In oblong baking dish, toss vegetables with Italian dressing.
2. Heat, covered, 9 to 10 minutes until vegetables are crisp-tender, stirring once.
   Chill before serving.

*Hint: *Choose a variety of vegetables that heat in about the same time (see Vegetable Chart). If using vegetables with different cooking times, cut vegetables with shorter cooking time into larger pieces.*

TEXAS STYLE NACHOS

Approx. Cooking Time: 3 min.
Yield: 20

Corn, taco or tortilla chips
Canned bean dip
Guacamole dip (optional)
Jalapeno Peppers, sliced (optional)
Shredded Monterey jack cheese

1. Spread 20 chips with bean dip and guacamole dip; top with peppers and cheese.
2. Arrange on serving plate. Heat 2 to 3 minutes until cheese is melted; serve immediately. Repeat procedure as desired.

BLUE CHEESE SPREAD

Approx. Cooking Time: 5 min.
Yield: 3 cups

- **1 envelope unflavored gelatin**
- **3/4 cup water**
- **1 tablespoon lemon juice**
- **1 package (3 oz.) cream cheese, softened**
- **1/3 cup milk**
- **1/4 pound blue cheese, crumbled**
- **1/2 cup sour cream**
- **1/4 cup diced green pepper or finely chopped walnuts**
- **2 teaspoons Worcestershire sauce**

1. In small glass bowl, sprinkle unflavored gelatin over water. Heat 4 to 5 minutes until gelatin is dissolved, stirring twice. Add lemon juice; cool slightly.
2. In medium bowl, blend cream cheese and milk until smooth; stir in blue cheese, sour cream, green pepper, Worcestershire and gelatin mixture.
3. Turn into 3-cup mold or bowl and chill until firm.
4. Unmold and serve with crackers as a spread.

CRAZY MIX

Approx. Cooking Time: 8 to 9 min.
Yield: 2 quarts

- **1/2 cup butter or margarine**
- **2 tablespoons Worcestershire sauce**
- **1/2 teaspoon garlic salt**
- **1/2 teaspoon salt**
- **2 cups bite-size crispy corn squares**
- **2 cups bite-size crispy rice squares**
- **2 cups bite-size crispy wheat squares**
- **1 cup salted peanuts**
- **1 cup thin pretzel sticks**

1. In 3-qt. casserole, heat butter 2 to 2½ minutes until melted.
2. Stir in Worcestershire, garlic and salt. Add remaining ingredients, stirring well.
3. Heat 6 to 7 minutes until butter is absorbed and mixture is crispy, stirring every 3 minutes. Cool before serving or storing.

SPICED ALMONDS

Approx. Cooking Time: 9 min.
Yield: 2 cups

- **2 tablespoons butter or margarine**
- **1 to 2 teaspoons curry powder**
- **1 tablespoon Worcestershire sauce**
- **2 cups blanched almonds**

1. In oblong baking dish, heat butter 1 minute until melted.
2. Stir in curry powder and Worcestershire sauce.
3. Add almonds and coat thoroughly. Heat 6 to 8 minutes, stirring twice; cool.

Variations:
For CHILI CASHEWS, *stir 1 to 2 teaspoons chili powder and 2 cups salted cashews into melted butter.*

For GINGER WALNUTS, *stir 1 to 2 teaspoons ground ginger, 1 tablespoon soy sauce and 2 cups walnuts into melted butter.*

STUFFED MUSHROOMS

Approx. Cooking Time: 25 min.
Yield: 24 mushrooms

- **1 pound medium fresh mushrooms (about 24), cleaned**
- **4 slices bacon, cut in 1-inch pieces**
- **1/4 cup finely chopped onion**
- **1 cup soft bread crumbs**
- **1/4 cup grated Parmesan cheese**
- **1/4 teaspoon pepper**

1. Remove mushroom stems and finely chop 1 cup; reserve.
2. In medium glass bowl, heat bacon and onion 4½ to 5 minutes until bacon is crisp, stirring once; drain.
3. Stir in reserved mushroom stems, bread crumbs, cheese and pepper.
4. Stuff mushroom caps with bread crumb mixture and arrange 12 in circular pattern on glass platter. Heat, covered, 9 to 10 minutes, giving dish ¼ turn after 4 minutes. Let stand, uncovered, 3 minutes before serving; repeat procedure.

Variation:
For SPINACH STUFFED MUSHROOMS *partially thaw 1 package (12 oz.) frozen spinach souffle. Cut into squares and place in mushroom caps; sprinkle, if desired, with onion salt. Heat as directed above.*

Memo

Pictured on the following page: Pepper Steak ▶

SPECIAL HINTS FOR ROASTING MEATS

- Place roast on microwave oven safe roasting rack in a shallow baking dish. If this specially designed rack is unavailable, an inverted saucer or casserole lid works well in holding the roast out of its juices.
- Loosely cover the baking dish with wax paper to prevent spattering.
- After approximately half of cooking time, turn roast over top to bottom.
- Cover less meaty portions of meats with small pieces of aluminum foil half way through cooking to prevent over-cooking of these areas. Wooden toothpicks can be used to hold the foil in place.

- Let stand, covered, 10 to 15 minutes after cooking. This time allows the temperature to equalize throughout. The internal temperature will rise 5°F to 10°F ... a good time to prepare gravy or a vegetable.
- Use a cooking bag or covered casserole when cooking less tender cuts of meat (pot roast, etc.) These should be covered by liquid (soup, broth, etc.) to help foods retain moisture, producing a tender, juicy roast.
- Prepare cooking bag as package directs. Do not use twist ties to close bag. Slash bag near closure to allow excess steam to escape.

MEAT ROASTING CHART

Cut	Weight	*Internal Temp.	Approximate Time; per lb.
BEEF			
Standing Rib Roast	5 lbs.	125°F Rare	7-8 min.
		145°F Med.	8-9 min.
		160°F Well	11-13 min.
Sirloin Tip	4 lbs.	125°F Rare	7-8 min.
		145°F Med.	9-10 min.
		160°F Well	12-13 min.
PORK			
Rolled, Boneless	3 to 4 lbs.	170°F Well	12 min.
Loin roast bone-in	3 to 4 lbs.	170°F Well Add ¼ cup water to dish. Cover loosely with plastic wrap.	12-13 min.
Ribs	2 to 4 lbs.		15-17 min.
HAM			
Canned precooked. Reheating only	5 lbs.	115°F Add ¼ cup water to dish. Cover loosely with plastic wrap. Edges and fatty areas may need to be shielded with strips of foil.	8-9 min.

*Degree of doneness is the internal temperature of roast when taken from oven. Another 5°F to 10°F increase will occur as meat stands 10 to 15 minutes prior to carving.

TIPS FOR PREPARING CONVENIENCE MEATS

- A variety of meats, especially bacon, may be cooked between layers of paper towels to prevent oven spatter.

- Cover meats with wax paper to prevent oven spatter.
- After cooking, let stand, covered, 1 to 3 minutes before serving.

ITEM	AMT.	COOK TIME (in min.)
Beef Patties, frozen	1	3 to 4
(3½ oz. ea.)	2	5 to 6
	4	7 to 9
Bacon, slices	2	1 to 2
	3	2 to 3
	4	4 to 5
	8	6 to 8
Canadian bacon, slices	2	1 to 2
(2 oz. ea.)	4	3 to 4
	8	4 to 6
Frankfurters, scored	2	1 to 2
	4	3 to 4
Hamburgers	1	1 to 2
(4 oz. ea.)	2	2 to 3
	4	5 to 6
Sausage Links, frozen	2	1 to 2
(precooked, brown	4	3 to 4
and serve)	8	5 to 6
** Sausage Links, fresh	2	3 to 4
(1 to 2 oz. ea.)	4	5 to 6
	8	7 to 8
Sausage Patties, fresh	2	3 to 4
(1 to 2 oz. ea.)	4	6 to 7

**Meat covered with casings must be pierced with a fork prior to heating to prevent bursting. It is also advisable to brush with a browning sauce before cooking.*

ITALIAN MEATBALLS

Approx. Cooking Time: 12 min.
Yield: 4 servings

- **1 pound ground beef**
- **1 egg**
- **1 1/2 cups soft bread crumbs**
- **1/4 cup water or milk**
- **2 to 3 tablespoons grated Parmesan cheese**
- **3/4 teaspoon oregano**
- **1 teaspoon parsley**
- **1 teaspoon onion salt**

1. Combine all ingredients and shape into 1 1/2-inch meatballs (about 20).
2. Arrange in 10 x 6 x 2-inch baking dish and heat 10 to 12 minutes, draining liquid and rearranging meatballs once.

CHEESEBURGER PIE

Approx. Cooking Time: 22 to 24 min.
Yield: 6 servings

- **1 pound ground beef**
- **1 package (5 oz.) instant mashed potato flakes (2 1/4 cups)**
- **1 1/4 cups milk**
- **1 egg**
- **1/4 cup catsup**
- **1 tablespoon dried onion flakes**
- **1 1/2 teaspoons salt**
- **1/4 teaspoon pepper**
- **6 slices American cheese**
- **1 cup hot water**
- **2 tablespoons butter or margarine**

1. Combine ground beef, 1 cup instant mashed potato flakes, 1 cup milk, egg, catsup, onion, 1 teaspoon salt and 1/8 teaspoon pepper. Spread into 9-inch glass pie plate. Cover with wax paper.
2. Heat 14 to 16 minutes, giving dish 1/4 turn every 4 minutes.
3. Arrange 2 slices cheese on top. Let stand loosely covered. 10 minutes.
4. In medium glass bowl, heat water, butter, remaining milk, salt and pepper 7 to 8 minutes. Add remaining instant mashed potato flakes and diced cheese. Stir until potatoes are fluffy. Spread over "cheeseburger".
5. Heat 5 to 6 minutes until heated through, giving dish 1/4 turn after 3 minutes.

PIZZA WHEELS

Approx. Cooking Time: 8 min.
Yield: 4 servings

- **1 pound ground beef**
- **2 tablespoons finely chopped onion**
- **1/2 teaspoon salt**
  Oregano
- **1/4 cup spaghetti sauce**
- **4 slices Mozzarella cheese, cut into strips**

1. Combine ground beef, onion, salt and 1/4 teaspoon oregano; shape into 4 patties raising the edge 1/4 inch to form a center well. In baking dish, arrange patties; heat 4 to 5 1/2 minutes. Drain.
2. Fill center well with spaghetti sauce and sprinkle with oregano; heat 1 to 2 minutes. Top with cheese and let stand, covered, 4 minutes before serving.

Note: **For TWO servings,** *follow above procedure; halve all ingredients. Heat patties 2 to 3 minutes and with sauce 1 to 1 1/2 minutes.*

ORIENTAL PEPPER BURGERS

Approx. Cooking Time: 17 min.
Yield: 4 servings

- **1 pound ground beef**
- **1/4 teaspoon salt**
- **1/8 teaspoon pepper**
- **1 large onion, sliced**
- **1 medium green pepper, cut into chunks**
- **1 can (8 oz.) tomato sauce**
- **1/4 teaspoon ground ginger**
- **4 teaspoons soy sauce**

1. Combine beef, salt and pepper; shape into 4 patties and arrange in baking dish. Heat 6 to 8 minutes, drain.
2. Add onion, green pepper and tomato sauce blended with ginger and soy sauce.
3. Heat, covered, 8 to 9 minutes until vegetables are tender. Let stand, covered, 5 minutes before serving.

TINY MEAT LOAF

Approx. Cooking Time: 22 min.
Yield: 4 servings

- **1 pound ground beef**
- **1 egg**
- **1/3 cup dry bread crumbs**
- **1/3 cup catsup**
- **2 tablespoons milk or water**
- **2 envelopes (1/4 oz. ea.) instant onion soup**

1. Combine all ingredients and mold into a rounded flat loaf in 9-inch pie plate.
2. Heat 15 to 17 minutes, giving dish 1/4 turn every 5 minutes. Let stand about 10 minutes to firm before serving.

SWEDISH MEATBALLS

Approx. Cooking Time: 15 min.
Yield: 4 to 6 servings

- **1 pound ground beef**
- **1 egg**
- **1/2 cup dry bread crumbs**
- **1/2 cup milk**
- **1/4 cup finely chopped onion**
- **2 teaspoons parsley flakes**
- **1/2 teaspoon salt**
- **1/8 teaspoon ground allspice**
- **1/8 teaspoon pepper**
- **1 can (10 3/4 oz.) condensed cream of mushroom soup**

1. Combine ground beef, egg, bread crumbs, 1/4 cup milk, onion, parsley, salt, allspice and pepper. Shape into 1 1/4-inch meatballs (about 20) and arrange in oblong baking dish. Heat 8 to 9 minutes, rearranging meatballs after 5 minutes.
2. Blend soup with remaining milk; pour over meatballs. Heat, covered, 4 to 6 minutes until heated through.
Serve over buttered noodles.

STUFFED GREEN PEPPERS

Approx. Cooking Time: 30 min.
Yield: 4 servings

- **1 pound ground beef**
- **1/3 cup finely chopped onion**
- **2 cans (8 oz. ea.) tomato sauce**
- **1/4 cup water**
- **3 tablespoons grated Parmesan cheese**
- **1 teaspoon salt**
- **1/8 teaspoon pepper**
- **1/2 cup packaged precooked rice**
- **4 medium green peppers (about 1 lb.)**

1. In medium glass bowl, crumble ground beef; stir in onion. Heat 5 to 7 minutes until beef is brown, stirring once; drain.
2. Stir in 1 can tomato sauce, water, 1 tablespoon cheese, salt and pepper. Heat, covered, 3 to 5 minutes. Stir in rice; let stand, covered 10 minutes.
3. Cut off tops of peppers; remove seeds and rinse. Spoon beef-rice filling into each pepper; place in 2-qt casserole. Top with remaining sauce and cheese.
4. Heat, covered, 15 to 18 minutes until peppers are tender. Let stand, covered, 5 minutes before serving.

SALISBURY STEAK

Approx. Cooking Time: 24 min.
Yield: 6 servings

- **1 1/2 pounds ground beef**
- **1 can (10 3/4 oz.) condensed cream of mushroom soup**
- **1 can (4 oz.) mushrooms pieces, drained**
- **1 egg**
- **3/4 cup milk**
- **1/2 cup dry bread crumbs**
- **1/4 cup finely chopped onion**
- **1/8 teaspoon pepper**

1. Combine ground beef, 1/4 cup soup, 1/2 mushrooms, egg, 1/4 cup milk, bread crumbs, onion and pepper. Shape into 6 patties and arrange in 10 x 6 x 2-inch baking dish. Heat, covered with wax paper, 18 to 19 minutes, giving dish 1/2 turn after 9 minutes.
2. Drain and let stand, covered 5 minutes. In small glass bowl, combine remaining soup, mushrooms and milk; heat 3 to 4 minutes, stirring once.
3. Pour sauce over patties and garnish, if desired, with parsley.

BEEF WITH BROCCOLI

Approx. Cooking Time: 25 min.
Yield: 4 servings

- **1 tablespoon oil**
- **1 pound boneless steak, cut into thin strips**
- **1 clove garlic, finely chopped**
- **1/8 teaspoon ground ginger**
- **3 to 4 cups broccoli flowerets**
- **1 tablespoon cornstarch**
- **1 tablespoon sherry**
- **1 tablespoon soy sauce**
  Toasted sesame seeds

1. In 10 x 6 x 2-inch baking dish, heat oil 3 minutes.
2. Stir in beef, garlic and ginger; heat an additional 5 to 7 minutes, stirring twice.
3. Add broccoli and heat, covered, 8 to 9 minutes until broccoli is crisp tender, stirring once.
4. Stir in cornstarch blended with sherry and soy sauce; heat 4 1/2 to 6 minutes until sauce is thickened, stirring once. Top with sesame seeds.

SAVORY CABBAGE ROLLS

Approx. Cooking Time: 26 min.
Yield: 4 servings

- **1 small head cabbage (about 1 1/2 lbs).**
- **1 pound ground beef**
- **3/4 cup chopped onion**
- **1 can (15 oz.) tomato sauce**
- **1/2 cup cooked rice**
- **1 teaspoon salt**
- **1/8 teaspoon pepper**
- **2 tablespoons brown sugar**
- **2 tablespoons cider vinegar**

1. Cut core from cabbage; rinse. In medium glass bowl, heat, covered, 6 to 8 minutes. Remove 8 leaves; reserve (use remaining cabbage in other recipes).
2. Into glass bowl, crumble ground beef: stir in onions. Heat 5 to 7 minutes until beef is browned, stirring once; drain. Stir in 1/2 tomato sauce, rice, salt and pepper.
3. Place beef-rice filling in cabbage leaf; roll up, folding edges in. Arrange seam-side down in square baking dish. Pour in remaining tomato sauce blended with brown sugar and vinegar.
4. Heat, covered, 9 to 11 minutes. Let stand, covered, 5 minutes before serving.

OVEN-FRIED PORK CHOPS

Approx. Cooking Time: 12 to 14 min.
Yield: 4 servings

- **4 rib pork chops, 1/2-inch thick**
- **1 package (1 3/8 oz.) seasoned coating mix for pork**

1. Coat chops according to package directions. Arrange chops in 8-inch square baking dish ribs toward center.
2. Heat 12 to 14 minutes giving dish 1/4 turn every 5 minutes. Let stand, covered, 5 minutes before serving.

COUNTRY STUFFED PORK CHOPS

Approx. Cooking Time: 19 min.
Yield: 4 servings

- **4 rib pork chops, ³/₄-in. thick**
  Pepper
- **¹/₂ cup finely chopped apple**
- **¹/₄ cup thinly sliced celery**
- **3 tablespoons raisins**
- **¹/₈ teaspoon ground cinnamon**
- **³/₄ cup apple juice**
  Browning sauce
- **2 tablespoons flour**
- **¹/₂ teaspoon salt**

1. Cut pocket in each chop; sprinkle inside with pepper. Combine apple, celery, raisins and cinnamon. Stuff each chop with apple mixture and secure opening with wooden toothpicks. In 8-inch square baking dish, arrange chops, ribs toward center, add ¹/₂ cup apple juice. Brush chops with browning sauce.
2. Heat, covered, 15 to 17 minutes basting chops once. Remove chops to serving platter; let stand, covered, 5 minutes.
3. Meanwhile, into baking dish, stir flour blended with remaining apple juice and salt. Heat 2 minutes until thickened, stirring once. Serve over chops.

CHINESE PORK AND GREEN VEGETABLES

Approx. Cooking Time: 20 min.
Yield: 4 servings

- **2 tablespoons oil**
- **1 pound boneless pork, cut into thin strips**
- **2 tablespoons soy sauce**
- **¹/₈ teaspoon garlic powder**
- **1 package (6 oz.) frozen pea pods, thawed**
- **2 bunches green onions, cut into ³/₄-inch pieces (about ²/₃ cup)**
- **2 tablespoons cornstarch**
- **1 cup beef broth**

1. In 10 x 6 x 2-inch baking dish, heat oil 3 minutes, stir in pork, soy sauce and garlic. Heat 5 to 7 minutes, stirring occasionally.

2. Add pea pods and green onions; heat, covered, 4 minutes, stirring once. Stir in cornstarch blended with broth and heat 4 to 6 minutes until sauce is slightly thickened, stirring occasionally. Serve over rice.

POLISH SAUSAGE (KIELBASA) WITH RED CABBAGE

Approx. Cooking Time: 31 min.
Yield: 6 servings

- **1 small head red cabbage (about 2 lbs.), shredded ✱**
- **1 small apple, chopped**
- **¹/₄ cup sugar**
- **¹/₄ cup cider vinegar**
- **1 tablespoon dried onion flakes**
- **¹/₂ teaspoon caraway seeds**
- **¹/₂ teaspoon salt**
- **1 ring (1³/₄ to 2 lbs.) Kielbasa sausage**

1. In 2-qt casserole, combine cabbage, apple, sugar, vinegar, onion, caraway and salt. Heat, covered, 10 to 12 minutes, stirring every 3 minutes.
2. Make ¹/₄-inch slits every few inches in Kielbasa; arrange on red cabbage. Heat, covered, 18 to 19 minutes until heated through. Let stand, covered, 5 minutes before serving.

✱Substitution: *Use 2 jars (16 oz. ea.) red cabbage, drained for fresh cabbage. Do not heat cabbage separately. Arrange Kielbasa on red cabbage blended with remaining ingredients. Heat, covered, 22 to 25 minutes until heated through.*

SWEET AND SOUR PORK

Approx. Cooking Time: 20 min.
Yield: 4 servings

- **1 can (8¼ oz.) pineapple chunks in heavy syrup, drained (reserve ⅓ cup syrup)**
- **¼ cup cider vinegar**
- **1 tablespoon cornstarch**
- **2 tablespoons oil**
- **1 pound boneless pork, cut into ¾-inch cubes**
- **¼ cup soy sauce**
- **1 bunch green onions, thinly sliced**
- **1 green pepper, cut into small chunks**

1. In small glass bowl, combine reserved syrup, vinegar and cornstarch; heat 1 to 2 minutes until thickened, stirring once.
2. In 8-inch square baking dish, heat oil 3 minutes; stir in pork, soy sauce and onion. Heat 10 to 11 minutes, stirring twice.
3. Add green pepper and pineapple; heat, covered, 3 to 4 minutes or until pork is tender.
4. Stir in sauce and let stand, covered, 5 minutes before serving.

WURST WITH KRAUT

Approx. Cooking Time: 26 min.
Yield: 6 servings

- **6 tablespoons butter or margarine**
- **1½ cups chopped onion (about 2 medium)**
- **2 cups sliced apples (about 2 medium)**
- **2 cans (16 oz. ea.) sauerkraut, drained and rinsed**
- **½ cup beef broth**
- **¼ teaspoon caraway seeds**
- **¼ teaspoon pepper**
- **6 knockwurst sausages (about 3 oz. ea.)**

1. In 10 x 6 x 2-inch baking dish heat butter and onion 4 to 5 minutes. Stir in apples and heat 5 to 7 minutes. Stir in sauerkraut, broth, caraway and pepper.
2. Score knockwurst diagonally and arrange on sauerkraut mixture. Heat 12 to 14 minutes rearranging knockwurst after 6 minutes. Let stand, covered, 5 minutes.

VEAL CUTLETS CORDON BLEU

Approx. Cooking Time: 16 to 18 min.
Yield: 4 servings

- **4 veal cutlets (about ¾ lb.), pounded thin**
- **2 thin slices cooked ham, halved**
- **2 slices (rectangular) Swiss cheese, halved**
- **1 cup seasoned dry bread crumbs**
- **½ teaspoon salt**
- **⅛ teaspoon pepper Ground allspice**
- **1 egg, beaten with ¼ cup water**
- **2 tablespoons oil**

1. On one side of each cutlet, place ham and cheese; fold cutlet in half. Secure edges with wooden toothpicks. Dip cutlets in bread crumbs mixed with salt, pepper and allspice; dip in egg, then again in bread crumbs. Coat bottom of oblong baking dish with oil; place cutlets in dish.
2. Heat 16 to 18 minutes turning cutlets over and re-arranging after 8 minutes. Let stand, covered, with wax paper, 5 minutes before serving.

CURRY LAMB

Power Level: HIGH
　　　　　　DEFROST
Approx. Cooking Time: 26 min.
Yield: 4 servings

  **1　pound lamb, cut into 1 1/2-inch
　　pieces**
  3/4　cup finely chopped onion
  1/4　cup butter or margarine
  3　tablespoons flour
  1　cup chicken broth
  1/3　cup flaked coconut
  1/3　cup raisins or peanuts
  3　tablespoons lemon juice
  1　tablespoon lemon juice
  1　tablespoon curry powder
  1/2　teaspoon ground ginger
  1/2　teaspoon salt

1. In 2-quart casserole dish, heat lamb,
   onion and butter 7 to 9 minutes on HIGH,
   stirring once.
2. Stir in flour, then remaining ingredients.
   Heat, covered, 7 minutes on HIGH.
3. Continue cooking on DEFROST an additional 8 to 10 minutes until lamb is tender,
   stirring twice. Serve over rice.

PERSIAN LAMB WITH PEACHES

Power Level: HIGH-DEFROST-HIGH
Approx. Cooking Time: 32 min.
Yield: 6 servings

  Water
  **1　can (16 oz.) peach slices,
　　drained (reserve syrup)**
  **1 1/2　pounds boneless lamb, cut into
　　1 1/2-inch cubes**
  **1　envelope (1 oz.) onion-mushroom
　　soup mix**
  1　tablespoon lemon juice
  1/4　teaspoon ground cinnamon
  1/8　teaspoon ground cloves
  1/4　cup raisins
  2　tablespoons cornstarch
  1/4　cup water

1. Add enough water to reserved syrup to
   equal 1 cup. In 2-quart casserole dish,
   combine with lamb, soup mix, lemon
   juice, cinnamon and cloves. Heat, covered, 9 to 11 minutes on HIGH.

2. Continue cooking on DEFROST an additional 13 minutes until lamb is tender.
   Stir in peaches, raisins and cornstarch
   blended with 1/4 cup water.
3. Heat 6 to 8 minutes on HIGH until sauce
   is thickened, stirring once.

FLANK STEAK

Power Level: HIGH
　　　　　　DEFROST
Approx. Cooking Time: 28 min.
Yield: 4 servings

  1/4　pound fresh mushrooms
  1/2　cup finely chopped onion
  1　clove garlic, finely chopped
  2　tablespoons butter
  **1　package (10 oz.) frozen chopped
　　spinach, thawed and well
　　drained**
  1　beef flank steak (1 1/2 to 1 3/4 lbs.)
  2　beef bouillon cubes
  1　cup hot water
  **1　can (10 3/4 oz.) condensed cream
　　of mushroom soup**
  **2　tablespoons dry vermouth
　　(optional)**

1. Chop 1/2 cup mushrooms; in glass bowl,
   combine with onion, garlic and butter.
   Heat 3 to 4 minutes on HIGH until onion
   and mushrooms are tender; stir in spinach.
2. Pound flank steak with a mallet; spread
   spinach mixture on steak in a lengthwise
   strip. Roll steak lengthwise around filling;
   tie with string or secure with wooden
   toothpicks. Place steak roll in an 10 x 6 x
   2-inch baking dish.
3. Combine bouillon, water, soup and vermouth; add remaining mushrooms,
   sliced. Pour sauce over steak roll. Heat,
   covered, 12 to 14 minutes on HIGH.
4. Continue cooking on DEFROST an additional 8 to 10 minutes until beef is tender.
   Let stand, covered, 10 minutes before
   serving.

SOUTHERN BARBECUED RIBS

Approx. Cooking Time: 35 to 37 min.
Yield: 4 servings

- **2 pounds pork spareribs, cut into individual ribs**
- **1 cup barbecue sauce**
- **2 tablespoons honey or dark corn syrup**
- **2 tablespoons flour**
- **1 tablespoon soy sauce**

1. Arrange ribs in 10" x 6" x 2" dish with meaty portions toward outside of dish.
2. Combine remaining ingredients and pour over ribs. Cover loosely with plastic wrap.
3. Heat 35 to 37 minutes rearranging ribs top to bottom and end to end after 18 minutes.

PINEAPPLE HAM AND YAMS

Approx. Cooking Time: 12 to 14 min.
Yield: 4 servings

- **1 tablespoon butter**
- **1 can (8-oz.) yams or sweet potatoes, drained**
- **2 tablespoons brown sugar**
- **4 slices (about 4-oz.) packaged, thinly sliced cooked ham**
- **1 can (8-oz.) sliced pineapple (4 slices)**
- **1/4 cup coarsely chopped pecans**
- **1/4 cup brown sugar**
- **1/4 cup syrup reserved from pineapple**

1. In 1-qt. casserole place butter; heat 1 minute, to melt. Add drained yams and mash well. Stir in brown sugar. Divide mixture equally over one end of each ham slice. Roll up into firm rolls.
2. Drain pineapple, reserving juice. Place pineapple slices in 8-in square dish. Cover each with ham roll, seam side down.
3. Combine pecans, sugar and pineapple syrup. Spoon over ham rolls. Cover with wax paper.
4. Heat 12 to 14 minutes, giving dish 1/4 turn every 5 minutes.

VEAL PAPRIKA

Power Level: HIGH–DEFROST–HIGH
Approx. Cooking Time: 25 min.
Yield: 4 servings

- **1 pound veal, cut into 1-inch pieces**
- **1/2 pound fresh mushrooms, sliced**
- **1 cup chicken broth**
- **1/2 cup finely chopped onions**
- **1 teaspoon paprika**
- **1/2 teaspoon salt**
- **1/4 teaspoon pepper**
  Dash caraway seeds
- **3 tablespoons flour**
- **1/2 cup sour cream**

1. In 2-quart casserole , combine veal, mushrooms, 1/2 cup broth, onion, paprika, salt, pepper and caraway. Heat, covered, 8 minutes on HIGH.
2. Continue cooking on DEFROST an additional 10 to 12 minutes until veal is tender, stirring occasionally. Drain liquid and reserve 1/2 cup. Into dish, stir flour blended with remaining broth and reserved liquid.
3. Heat 3 to 5 minutes on HIGH until sauce is thickened; blend in sour cream.

Pictured on the following page: Roast Chicken ▶

SPECIAL HINTS FOR PREPARING POULTRY

For Whole Birds—Fresh or Thawed

- Stuff bird, if desired; close cavity with string or wooden toothpicks.
- Tie wings and legs tightly to body of bird.
- Place poultry, on microwave oven safe roasting rack in a shallow baking dish. If this specially designed rack is unavailable, an inverted saucer or casserole lid works well in holding the bird out of its juices.
- Brush bird with browning sauce before cooking to enhance appearance.
- Loosely cover baking dish with wax paper to prevent spattering.
- After approximately half of cooking time, give dish a half turn.
- Cover thin points (wings and legs) with strips of aluminum foil halfway through cooking to prevent overcooking in these areas.

- Let stand, covered, 10 to 15 minutes before serving. This time allows the temperature to equalize throughout. The internal temperature will rise 5° to 10°F ... a good time to prepare gravy or a vegetable.
- Use a cooking bag or covered casserole when cooking less tender hens. These should be covered with liquid (soup, broth, etc.) to help retain moisture, producing a tender, juicy bird.
- Prepare cooking bag as package directs. Do not use twist-ties. Slash bag near closure to allow excess steam to escape.

Note: *A thermometer may be used after cooking time is completed to check the internal temperature of the food. A microwave oven safe thermometer may be used during cooking. DO NOT use a conventional meat thermometer in poultry while operating the microwave oven.*

POULTRY ROASTING CHART

Type	Weight	Approx. Time per lb.
CHICKEN		
Whole, Fryer	2-3 lbs.	9 min.
Whole, Roaster	4-5 lbs.	9 min.
Parts	2 lbs. Approx. 6 pieces	8 min.
Cornish Game Hen	1-2 lbs.	9 min.
Duckling	4-5 lbs.	9 min.

Note: *Total cooking time is about the same for stuffed or unstuffed poultry. Times are approximate and may vary due to the starting temperature.*

BARBECUED CHICKEN

Approx. Cooking Time: 18 min.
Yield: 4 servings

- **2 to 2¹/₂ pounds chicken, cut into serving pieces**
- **1 cup barbecue sauce**

1. In 10 x 6 x 2-inch baking dish, arrange chicken, meatier portions toward edge of dish; spread sauce over chicken. Heat, covered with wax paper 16 to 18 minutes. Baste chicken with sauce once, and give dish ¹/₂ turn after 8 minutes.
2. Let stand, covered, 10 minutes before serving.

CHICKEN TERIYAKI

Approx. Cooking Time: 32 to 37 min.
Yield: 4 servings

- **¹/₄ cup soy sauce**
- **¹/₃ cup honey**
- **¹/₃ cup sherry**
- **1 whole chicken, about 2¹/₂ lbs.**

1. In 10 x 6 x 2-inch dish, mix soy sauce, honey and sherry.
2. Add chicken turning over and coating with sauce.
3. Cover with plastic wrap. Marinate in refrigerator 1 to 2 hours, turning chicken over after ¹/₂ of time.
4. To microwave, place bird breast side down in dish. Heat 30 to 34 minutes, turning breast side up, after 15 minutes. Let chicken stand 10 minutes before serving. Prepare Teriyaki sauce (below) and finish chicken as described in sauce recipe.

Teriyaki Sauce: *In 1-pt. glass measuring cup stir together 1 tablespoon water and 2 tablespoons cornstarch. Pour juices from cooking dish into cup. Heat 2 to 3 minutes, until thick and clear, stirring after 1 minute. Pour sauce over chicken just before serving.*

BUTTER BAKED CHICKEN

Approx. Cooking Time: 19 min.
Yield: 4 servings

- **2 to 2¹/₂ pounds chicken, cut into serving pieces**
- **3 tablespoons butter or margarine, melted**
- **1 teaspoon browning sauce**

1. In 10 x 6 x 2-inch baking dish, arrange chicken, meatier portions toward edge of dish. Combine butter and browning sauce and brush ¹/₂ mixture over chicken.
2. Heat, covered with wax paper, 16 to 19 minutes until chicken is tender; half way through cooking, brush remaining butter mixture on chicken.
3. Let stand, covered, 10 minutes before serving.

CHICKEN IN WINE SAUCE

Approx. Cooking Time: 21 min.
Yield: 4 servings

- **1 medium onion, sliced**
- **¹/₄ cup butter or margarine**
- **2 boneless chicken breasts, skinned and thinly sliced**
- **Salt and pepper to taste**
- **1 medium green pepper, cut into thin strips**
- **¹/₃ cup white wine**
- **1 jar (4¹/₂ oz.) sliced mushrooms, drained**
- **2 tablespoons flour**
- **²/₃ cup chicken broth**

1. In 10 x 6 x 2-inch baking dish, heat onion and butter 4 to 5 minutes until onion is tender. Add chicken and heat 4 to 5 minutes stirring once.
2. Season with salt and pepper; add green pepper and wine. Heat, covered, 3 to 5 minutes; add mushrooms and flour blended with broth. Heat 4 to 6 minutes until sauce is thickened, stirring twice.

CHICKEN CACCIATORE

Approx. Cooking Time: 19 min.
Yield: 4 servings

- **2 to 2¹/₂ pounds chicken, cut into serving pieces**
- **1 can (15 oz.) tomato sauce**
- **1 jar (4¹/₂ oz.) sliced mushrooms, drained**
- **¹/₂ cup chopped onion**
- **1 tablespoon sugar (optional)**
- **1 teaspoon oregano**
- **1 teaspoon salt**
- **¹/₂ teaspoon finely chopped garlic**
- **¹/₄ teaspoon pepper**

1. In 10 x 6 x 2-inch baking dish, arrange chicken. Combine remaining ingredients and spoon over chicken.
2. Heat, covered with wax paper, 16 to 19 minutes until chicken is tender, giving dish ¹/₂ turn after 8 minutes. Let stand, covered, 10 minutes. Serve with spaghetti.

WESTERN CHICKEN

Approx. Cooking Time: 20 min.
Yield: 4 servings

- **2 chicken breasts, split**
- **2 teaspoons lemon juice**
- **1 teaspoon dried onion flakes**
  Basil
  Pepper
- **²/₃ cup shredded Cheddar cheese**
- **¹/₂ small avocado, thinly sliced**
- **4 thin slices tomato**

1. In 8-inch square baking dish, arrange chicken; sprinkle with lemon juice and onion and season with basil and pepper.
2. Heat, covered with wax paper, 13 to 14 minutes until chicken is tender.
3. Top chicken with ¹/₂ cheese, avocado and tomato; top with remaining cheese.
4. Heat, covered, 5 to 6 minutes. Let stand 5 minutes before serving.

Note: For TWO servings, *follow above procedure; halve all ingredients. Heat chicken 9 to 9¹/₂ minutes and vegetables 2 to 3 minutes.*

HERB BAKED CHICKEN

Approx. Cooking Time: 19 min.
Yield: 4 servings

- **1 teaspoon garlic salt**
- **1 teaspoon paprika**
- **¹/₂ teaspoon oregano**
- **¹/₄ teaspoon pepper**
  Juice and grated peel of 1 lemon
- **2 to 2¹/₂ pounds chicken, cut into serving pieces**
- **1 jar (4¹/₂ oz.) sliced mushrooms, drained**

1. Combine garlic, paprika, oregano, pepper and lemon peel; rub over chicken. In 10 x 6 x 2-inch baking dish, arrange chicken, meatier portions toward edge of dish; drizzle with lemon juice and top with mushrooms.
2. Heat, covered with wax paper, 16 to 19 minutes until chicken is tender, giving dish ¹/₂ turn after 8 minutes. Let stand, covered, 5 minutes before serving.

HAWAIIAN CHICKEN

Approx. Cooking Time: 22 min.
Yield: 4 servings

- **2 to 2¹/₂ pounds chicken, cut into serving pieces**
- **2 tablespoons soy sauce**
- **¹/₄ teaspoon ground ginger**
- **1 green pepper, cut into chunks**
- **1 can (11 oz.) mandarin oranges, drained (reserve syrup)**
- **1 can (8¹/₄ oz.) pineapple slices, drained and halved (reserve syrup)**
- **1 tablespoon cornstarch**

1. In 10 x 6 x 2-inch baking dish, arrange chicken, meatier portions toward edge of dish; brush with soy sauce blended with ginger.
2. Add green pepper; heat, covered with wax paper, 16 to 19 minutes, drain. Let stand, covered, 10 minutes.
3. In 2-cup glass measure, blend cornstarch with 1 cup reserved syrups. Heat 3 minutes, stirring once.
4. Add fruit and pour over chicken.

CHICKEN WITH SNOW PEAS

Approx. Cooking Time: 20 min.
Yield: 6 servings

6 chicken thighs
1 tablespoon butter or margarine, melted
1 tablespoon soy sauce
1¹/₂ teaspoons paprika
¹/₂ teaspoon crushed rosemary
¹/₄ teaspoon salt
1 package (6 oz.) frozen pea pods, thawed
1 jar (2¹/₂ oz.) sliced mushrooms, drained

1. In 10 x 6 x 2-inch baking dish, arrange chicken. Combine butter, soy sauce, paprika, rosemary and salt; brush over chicken. Heat, covered with wax paper, 12 to 13 minutes.
2. Top with pea pods and mushrooms; heat, covered 5 to 7 minutes until chicken and vegetables are tender. Let stand, covered, 5 minutes before serving.

KABOBS IN JAM

Approx. Cooking Time: 13 min.
Yield: 4 servings

¹/₃ cup orange marmalade
2 tablespoons orange juice
2 tablespoons soy sauce
¹/₂ teaspoon lemon juice
Dash ground ginger
2 boneless chicken breasts, skinned and cut into 1¹/₂-inch pieces (about 1 to 1¹/₄ lbs.)
1 package (10 oz.) frozen Brussels sprouts, thawed

1. In medium glass bowl, heat marmalade, orange juice, soy sauce, lemon juice and ginger 3 to 4 minutes; add chicken and marinate 30 minutes.
2. On four 9 or 10-inch wooden skewers, alternately thread chicken and Brussels sprouts. Arrange skewers on 8-inch square baking dish and heat 7 to 9 minutes until chicken is tender, rearranging skewers once and brushing with marinade twice.

CHICKEN PARMESAN

Approx. Cooking Time: 18 min.
Yield: 4 servings

2 boneless chicken breasts, skinned, split and pounded thin
³/₄ cup seasoned dry bread crumbs
¹/₄ cup grated Parmesan cheese
¹/₄ teaspoon paprika
1 egg, beaten with ¹/₄ cup water
1 tablespoon oil
1 can (8 oz.) tomato sauce
Oregano
1 cup shredded Mozzarella cheese

1. Dip chicken in bread crumbs mixed with parmesan cheese and paprika, then in egg and again in bread crumb mixture.
2. Coat bottom of 10 x 6 x 2-inch baking dish with oil. Place chicken in dish. Heat 4 to 5 minutes; turn chicken over and heat an additional 4 to 5 minutes.
3. Top with tomato sauce and season with oregano; heat 6 to 8 minutes until sauce is hot. Sprinkle with mozzarella cheese and let stand, covered, 5 minutes or until cheese is melted.

Note: **For TWO servings,** *follow above procedure, halve all ingredients. Heat chicken 1¹/₂ to 2 minutes each side and with tomato sauce 3 to 3¹/₂ minutes.*

KOREAN CHICKEN AND CASHEWS

Approx. Cooking Time: 14 min.
Yield: 4 servings

>   3   **tablespoons oil**
>   2   **boneless chicken breasts, skinned and thinly sliced (about 1 to 1¼ lbs.)**
>   2   **cloves garlic, finely chopped**
>   2   **tablespoons soy sauce**
>   1   **tablespoon sherry**
>   1   **tablespoon cornstarch**
>   ¼   **teaspoon ground ginger**
>   1   **medium green pepper, cut into small chunks**
>   ½   **cup cashew halves**

1. In 10 x 6 x 2-inch baking dish, heat oil 3 minutes. Combine chicken, garlic, soy sauce, sherry, cornstarch and ginger.
2. Add to dish and heat 4 to 6 minutes, stirring twice. Add green pepper and cashews and heat, covered, 3 to 5 minutes until chicken and green pepper are tender, stirring once. Let stand 5 minutes before serving.

CURRY CHICKEN

Approx. Cooking Time: 19 min.
Yield: 4 servings

>   2   **to 2½ pounds chicken, cut into serving pieces**
>   1   **can (10¾ oz.) condensed cream of chicken soup**
>   1   **tomato, cut into wedges (optional)**
>   ½   **cup raisins or peanuts**
>   1   **tablespoon curry powder**
>   1   **tablespoon dried onion flakes**
>   ⅛   **teaspoon garlic powder**

1. In 10 x 6 x 2-inch baking dish, arrange chicken. Thoroughly combine remaining ingredients and spoon over chicken.
2. Heat, covered with wax paper, 16 to 19 minutes until chicken is tender, giving dish ½ turn after 8 minutes.
3. Let stand, covered, 10 minutes. Remove chicken to serving platter; stir sauce until smooth and serve over chicken.

CRISPY CHICKEN

Approx. Cooking Time: 19 min.
Yield: 4 servings

>   2   **to 2½ pounds chicken, cut into serving pieces**
>   1   **package (2⅜ oz.) seasoned coating mix for chicken**

1. Coat chicken according to package directions; arrange in 10 x 6 x 2-inch baking dish.
2. Heat, covered with wax paper, 16 to 19 minutes until chicken is tender, giving dish ½ turn after 8 minutes. Let stand 5 minutes before serving.

CONVENIENCE STUFFING MIXES

Approx. Cooking Time: 8 min.
Yield: 6 servings

>   1½   **to 1¾ cups hot water**
>   ¼   **cup butter**
>   1   **package (6 to 6½ oz.) stuffing mix with seasoning packet**

1. In 2-quart casserole dish, heat water, butter and seasoning packet 6 to 8 minutes; stir in stuffing crumbs.*
2. Let stand, covered, 5 minutes before serving.

This makes enough to stuff a 2½ to 3 pound bird.

Variations: *Add one of the following with seasoning packet:*
- *1 cup chopped fresh cranberries or apple.*
- *½ cup raisins, chopped nuts, or chopped apricots.*
- *½ pound browned sausage drained.*
- *1 can (8 oz.) whole kernel corn, drained.*

CRUMB COATED CHICKEN

Approx. Cooking Time: 15 to 17 min.
Yield: 4 servings

> 2 eggs
> 1/3 cup melted butter
> 1 teaspoon salt
> 1 1/2 cups buttery cracker crumbs (about 50)
> 2 chicken breasts, split, skin removed

1. In small bowl beat together eggs, butter and salt.
2. In shallow dish place crumbs. Coat chicken with crumbs, then egg mixture, then crumbs again.
3. Arrange chicken in 10 x 6 x 2-inch dish with meaty portions to outside edge of dish. Cover with wax paper.
4. Heat 15 to 17 minutes, giving dish 1/2 turn after 8 minutes. Let stand, covered, 5 minutes.

TURKEY DIVINE

Approx. Cooking Time: 20 min.
Yield: 4 servings

> 2 packages (10 oz. ea.) frozen broccoli spears, thawed
> 2 to 3 cups cut-up cooked turkey or chicken
> Salt and pepper to taste
> 1 can (11 oz.) condensed Cheddar cheese soup
> 1/2 cup milk
> 1/4 cup buttered bread crumbs
> 1/2 teaspoon paprika

1. In 10 x 6 x 2-inch baking dish, arrange broccoli; top with turkey. Heat, covered, 7 to 8 minutes, drain. Season with salt and pepper.
2. In small glass bowl, combine soup and milk. Heat 3 to 4 minutes, stir until smooth. Pour sauce over turkey; heat, covered, 7 to 8 minutes until heated thoroughly. Top with bread crumbs mixed with paprika; let stand, covered, 5 minutes before serving.

SPIRITED CHICKEN

Approx. Cooking Time: 19 min.
Yield: 6 servings

> 6 chicken legs
> 1/2 cup dry sherry
> 1/4 cup soy sauce
> 1 tablespoon Worcestershire sauce
> 1/2 teaspoon garlic powder

1. In 10 x 6 x 2-inch baking dish, combine all ingredients; marinate, 30 minutes.
2. Heat, covered with wax paper, 16 to 19 minutes until chicken is tender, rearranging chicken once. Let stand, covered, 10 minutes before serving.

CORNISH HENS WITH PEACH SAUCE

Approx. Cooking Time: 21 min.
Yield: 4 servings

> 2 cornish hens (about 1 lb. ea.), split
> Browning sauce
> Paprika
> Pepper
> 1 can (16 oz.) sliced peaches in heavy syrup, drained (reserve 1/3 cup syrup)
> 2/3 cup orange juice
> 1 tablespoon cornstarch
> 1/8 teaspoon ground ginger

1. In 10 x 6 x 2-inch baking dish, arrange hens; brush with browning sauce and season with paprika and pepper. Heat, covered with wax paper, 15 to 17 minutes until meat is tender, giving dish 1/2 turn after 8 minutes. Drain. Let stand, covered, 10 minutes.
2. In small glass bowl, combine reserved syrup, orange juice, cornstarch and ginger. Heat 2 to 3 minutes until sauce is thickened, stirring once.
3. Add peaches and spoon over hens. If necessary, heat 2 to 3 minutes before serving. Garnish, if desired, with slivered almonds.

BASIC BREAD STUFFING

Power Level: HIGH
DEFROST
Approx. Cooking Time: 16 min.
Yield: 6 to 8 servings (about 4 cups)

1 1/2 **cups thinly sliced celery**
  1 **cup chopped onion**
 1/2 **cup butter or margarine**
  8 **cups fresh bread cubes**
  2 **eggs**
 1/4 **cup water (optional)**
  3 **tablespoons parsley flakes**
  1 **to 1 1/2 teaspoons poultry**
   seasoning
  1 **teaspoon salt**
 1/2 **teaspoon pepper**

1. In 2-quart casserole dish, heat celery, onion and butter 9 to 10 minutes on HIGH, until celery and onion are tender, stirring twice. Add remaining ingredients; combine thoroughly.
2. Heat, covered, 4 to 6 minutes on DEFROST, until heated through.

This makes enough to stuff 2 (2 1/2 to 3 lb.) birds.

APPLE SAUSAGE STUFFING

Power Level: HIGH
DEFROST
Approx. Cooking Time: 19 min.
Yield: 8 servings (about 6 cups)

 1/2 **pound bulk pork sausage**
  1 **cup thinly sliced celery**
 1/2 **cup finely chopped onion**
  5 **cups fresh bread cubes**
  3 **cups chopped apple (3 medium)**
  2 **eggs, beaten**
  1 **to 1 1/2 teaspoons salt**
 1/4 **to 1/2 teaspoon poultry season-**
   ing

1. In 10 x 6 x 2-inch baking dish, crumble sausage; stir in celery and onion. Heat 6 to 8 minutes on   until sausage is browned, stirring twice; drain.

2. Add remaining ingredients; combine thoroughly. Heat, covered, 4 to 6 minutes on HIGH, giving dish 1/4 turn after 3 minutes.
3. Continue cooking on DEFROST an additional 4 to 4 1/2 minutes until heated through.

This makes enough to stuff a 7 to 9 pound bird.

CORN BREAD STUFFING

Approx. Cooking Time: 22 to 24 min.
Yield: 12 servings (about 9 cups)

1 1/2 **cups thinly sliced celery**
  1 **cup chopped onion**
 1/2 **cup butter or margarine**
  2 **packages (12 oz. ea.) corn bread**
   or corn muffin mix, baked and
   crumbled
  2 **eggs**
1 1/2 **cups orange juice or chicken**
   broth
1 1/2 **teaspoons salt**
 3/4 **teaspoon sage**
 1/4 **teaspoon pepper**

1. In 3-quart casserole, heat celery, onion and butter 14 minutes on HIGH until celery and onion are tender, stirring every 4 minutes. Add remaining ingredients; combine thoroughly.
2. Heat, covered, 8 to 10 minutes on DEFROST until heated through. Let stand, covered, 5 minutes before serving.

Pictured on the following page: Bouillabaisse ▶

BAKED STUFFED LOBSTER TAILS

Approx. Cooking Time: 10 min.
Yield: 2 servings

>   2 **lobster tails (about 8 oz. ea.)**
> 1 1/2 **tablespoons butter or**
>   **margarine, melted**
>   1/4 **cup seasoned dry bread crumbs**
>   1/8 **teaspoon onion powder**
>   1/8 **teaspoon paprika**
>   1/8 **teaspoon salt**

1. With kitchen shears, cut lobster through center of soft shell (underneath) to the tail. Lift lobster out of shell by loosening with fingers, leaving meat attached to tail section. (Lobster meat will rest on shell). Arrange in oblong baking dish.
2. Combine remaining ingredients; sprinkle over lobster. Heat, covered with wax paper 6 to 7 minutes until lobster is done. Let stand 5 minutes; serve, if desired, with Lemon Butter.

Lemon Butter:
In small glass bowl, Heat 1/2 cup butter and 1 to 2 tablespoons lemon juice 1 to 1 1/2 minutes until butter is melted.

HOT TUNA SALAD

Approx. Cooking Time: 10 to 13 min.
Yield: 6 servings

>   2 **cans (7 oz. ea.) tuna, drained**
>   2 **cups chopped celery**
>   2 **cups croutons, divided**
>   1 **cup mayonnaise**
>   1/2 **cup whole almonds**
>   1 **tablespoon finely chopped onion**
>   1 **tablespoon lemon juice**
>   1/2 **teaspoon salt**
>   1/2 **cup shredded Cheddar cheese**

1. In 2-quart casserole, mix together tuna, celery, 1 cup croutons, mayonnaise, almonds, onion, lemon juice and salt. Cover.
2. Heat for 10 minutes, giving dish 1/4 turn after 5 minutes.
3. Sprinkle with cheese and remaining croutons. Heat for 2 to 3 minutes until cheese melts.

BAKED SNAPPER A LA ORANGE

Approx. Cooking Time: 30 min.
Yield: 4 servings

>   1 **medium orange**
>   6 **tablespoons butter or margarine**
>   1 **small onion, finely chopped**
>   1 **tablespoon parsley flakes**
>   1/2 **teaspoon basil**
>   1/8 **teaspoon pepper**
>   2 **cups soft bread crumbs (about 4**
>   **slices bread)**
>   2 **whole red snapper (1 1/4 to 1 1/2**
>   **lbs. ea.) dressed and heads**
>   **removed**
>   **Salt**
>   1 **can (6 oz.) frozen orange juice**
>   **concentrate, thawed**

1. Slice 1/2 orange; peel and chop remaining half. In small glass bowl, heat butter, onion, parsley, basil and pepper 3 1/2 to 4 1/2 minutes until onion is tender; stir in bread crumbs and chopped orange.
2. In oblong baking dish, arrange fish; season inside with salt. Stuff cavity with bread crumb mixture. Heat, covered with wax paper, 19 1/2 to 22 1/2 minutes until fish is tender.
3. Pour orange juice over fish; add orange slices. Heat, covered with wax paper, 3 minutes. Let stand, covered, 4 1/2 minutes before serving.

FLOUNDER WITH SHRIMP SAUCE

Approx. Cooking Time: 12 min.
Yield: 4 servings

>   4 **flounder fillets (about 1/4 lb. ea.)**
>   1 **can (10 3/4 oz.) condensed cream**
>   **of shrimp soup**
>   1/4 **cup white wine or milk**
>   1/2 **cup shredded Swiss cheese**
>   **Parsley or slivered almonds**

1. Roll up fillets and arrange seam-side down in square baking dish. Combine soup, wine and cheese, spoon over fillets. Heat, covered, 11 to 12 minutes until fish is done.
2. Let stand, covered, 5 minutes; sprinkle with parsley before serving.

Hint: *When rolling-up fillets, place a thin strip of Swiss cheese in center.*

COQUILLE NEWFOUNDLAND

Approx. Cooking Time: 13 min.
Yield: 4 servings

- 1/4 **cup white wine**
- 1 **pound sea scallops**
- 2 **tablespoons butter or margarine**
- 1 **tablespoon dried onion flakes**
- 2 **tablespoons flour**
  Dash white pepper
- 3/4 **cup light cream or milk**
- 1 **jar (2 1/2 oz.) sliced mushrooms, drained**
- 1/3 **cup shredded Swiss cheese**
- 1/4 **cup buttered bread crumbs**
  Parsley flakes

1. In 8-inch round baking dish, pour wine over scallops; heat, coverd, 5 to 6 minutes until scallops are tender, stirring once.
2. Drain liquid and reserve 1/4 cup; let scallops stand, covered. In medium glass bowl, heat butter and onion 1 minute, stir in flour and pepper.
3. Gradually add cream and reserved liquid, stirring until smooth. heat 3 to 4 minutes until mixture is thickened, stirring twice. Stir in mushrooms and cheese; add scallops. Spoon mixture into 4 individual glass ramekins or serving dishes, top with bread crumbs and parsley.
4. Arrange ramekins on glass oven tray, heat 1 to 2 minutes until heated through.

POACHED FISH

Approx. Cooking Time: 10 min.
Yield: 3 servings

- **Butter or margarine**
- 1 **pound fish fillets**
  Salt and pepper to taste
- 2 **tablespoons onion, finely chopped**
- 1/2 **cup dry white wine**

1. Lightly butter a shallow baking dish and place fillets in dish. Sprinkle with salt, pepper and onions. Pour white wine over fish.
2. Cover tightly with plastic wrap and heat for 6 to 9 minutes until fish flakes. Baste with white wine and onions several times during cooking.

SALMON ROMANOFF

Approx. Cooking Time: 12 min.
Yield: 4 to 6 servings

- 1 **can (16 oz.) salmon, drained and flaked**
- 1 **package (8. oz.) medium egg noodles, cooked and drained**
- 1 1/2 **cups cottage cheese**
- 1 1/2 **cups sour cream**
- 1 **can (4 oz.) sliced mushrooms, drained**
- 1/2 **cup shredded Cheddar cheese**
- 2 **teaspoons dried onion flakes**
- 2 **teaspoons Worcestershire sauce**
- 1/2 **teaspoon salt**
- 1/8 **teaspoon dried garlic pieces**
  Shredded Cheddar cheese or buttered bread crumbs
  Paprika

1. In 3-quart casserole dish, thoroughly combine salmon, noodles, cottage cheese, sour cream, mushrooms, 1/2 cup cheese, onion, Worcestershire, salt and garlic. Heat, covered, 10 to 12 minutes until heated through, stirring twice.
2. Top with shredded cheese and sprinkle with paprika. Let stand, covered, 5 minutes before serving.

PARCHMENT SEAFOOD SPECTACULAR

Approx. Cooking Time: 13 min.
Yield: 4 servings

> **4 halibut or other seafood steaks (about 6 oz. ea.)**
> **2 tablespoons brandy**
> **1 tablespoon lemon juice**
> **2 tablespoons butter or margarine**
> **2 tablespoons dried chives**
> **Salt and pepper to taste**
> **1 cup sliced fresh mushrooms (about 1/4 lb.)**
> **1 small apple, thinly sliced**

1. For each serving, place fish on 10 x 15-inch piece parchment paper. Combine brandy and lemon juice; brush on fish. Dot each with butter, chives and season with salt and pepper.
2. Mound mushrooms and apple on top; bring paper up around fish. Fold edges over twice to seal top; fold side edges up. Place on glass oven tray, heat 11 to 13 1/2 minutes. Serve packet directly on dinner plate.

CLAM STUFFING

Approx. Cooking Time: 6 min.
Yield: 4 servings

> **2 cups seasoned croutons, crushed**
> **1 can (7 1/2 oz.) minced clams**
> **2 tablespoons grated Parmesan cheese**
> **1/2 teaspoon dried onion flakes**
> **1/8 teaspoon garlic powder**
> **Dash pepper**
> **1 tablespoon butter or margarine, melted**
> **1/2 tablespoon parsley flakes**

1. Reserve 1/4 cup crouton crumbs. Combine remaining crouton crumbs, clams, cheese, onion, garlic and pepper.
2. Spoon mixture into 4 individual glass baking shells or 6-ounce custard cups; top with reserved crumbs blended with butter and parsley.
3. Heat 4 to 6 minutes until heated through, rearranging dishes once.

TROUT AMANDINE

Approx. Cooking Time: 17 min.
Yield: 2 to 4 servings

> **1/3 cup butter or margarine**
> **1/2 cup slivered almonds**
> **2 whole trout, cleaned (about 12 oz. ea.)**
> **Salt and pepper to taste**
> **Lemon juice**

1. In 2-cup glass measure, heat butter and almonds 4 to 6 minutes until almonds are lightly browned, stirring twice.
2. In 10 x 6 x 2-inch baking dish, arrange fish; season inside of fish with salt, pepper and lemon juice. Pour butter and almonds inside and over fish. Heat, covered with wax paper, 9 to 11 minutes until fish is tender. Let stand, covered, 5 minutes before serving.

OYSTERS ROCKEFELLER EN CASSEROLE

Approx. Cooking Time: 20 min.
Yield: 4 servings

> **1 can (10 1/2 oz.) condensed oyster stew**
> **3 tablespoons flour**
> **2/3 cup shredded Cheddar cheese**
> **1 tablespoon dried onion flakes**
> **1 bay leaf, crushed**
> **2 package (10 oz. ea.) frozen chopped spinach, thawed**
> **1 pint large oysters, drained**
> **1/2 cup dry bread crumbs**
> **1/4 cup grated Parmesan cheese**
> **2 tablespoons butter or margarine, melted**
> **1/2 teaspoon paprika**

1. In medium glass bowl, combine stew, flour, cheddar cheese, onion and bay leaf; heat 4 to 5 minutes until sauce is thickened, stirring every minute.
2. In 2-quart casserole dish, spread spinach; pour on stew mixture. With toothpick pierce each oyster several times and arrange on stew. Top with bread crumbs mixed with parmesan cheese, butter and paprika.
3. Heat, uncovered, 7 minutes, giving dish 1/4 turn after 3 minutes. Cover dish and continue cooking 6 to 8 minutes, giving dish 1/4 turn after 3 minutes. Let stand, covered, 5 minutes.

SALMON STEAKS WITH DILL

Approx. Cooking Time: 15 min.
Yield: 4 servings

- 1/2 **cup thinly sliced celery**
- 1/4 **cup butter or margarine**
- 1/2 **tablespoon parsley flakes**
- 1 **teaspoon salt**
- 1/2 **teaspoon dill weed**
- 1/4 **teaspoon pepper**
- 1/4 **cup white wine**
- 4 **salmon steaks (about 4 oz. ea.)**

1. In 10 x 6 x 2-inch baking dish, combine celery, butter, parsley, salt, dill and pepper. Heat 4 to 6 minutes until celery is tender; stir in wine.
2. Arrange salmon in dish; spoon wine and butter mixture over salmon.
3. Heat, covered, with wax paper, 6 to 8 minutes until salmon is done. Let stand, covered, 5 minutes before serving.

SEAFOOD NEWBURG

Approx. Cooking Time: 10 min.
Yield: 4 servings

- 1 **can (10³/₄ oz.) condensed cream of mushroom soup**
- 1 **package (10 oz.) frozen peas, thawed**
- 1/4 **cup milk**
- 1 **pound seafood, cooked and cut into bite-size pieces**
- 1 **jar (2¹/₂ oz.) sliced mushrooms, drained**
- 2 **to 3 tablespoons sherry**

1. In 1¹/₂-quart casserole dish, combine soup, peas and milk. Heat, covered, 4 to 5 minutes, stirring once.
2. Add remaining ingredients. Heat, covered, 4 to 5 minutes until heated through, stirring once. Let stand, covered, 5 minutes before serving.

BOUILLABAISSE

Power Level: HIGH—DEFROST
                   HIGH
Approx. Cooking Time: 43 min.
Yield: 6 servings

- 1 **medium onion, sliced**
- 2 **tablespoons oil**
- 2 **cloves garlic, finely chopped**
- 6 **small clams, scrubbed (littleneck)**
- 1 **can (28 oz.) whole tomatoes, chopped**
- 2 **bottles (8 oz. ea.) clam juice**
- 2 **bay leaves**
- 1/2 **teaspoon salt**
- 1/8 **teaspoon pepper**
  Dash thyme
  Pinch saffron (optional)
- 1/2 **pound sea scallops**
- 1/2 **pound sole fillet, cut into 1¹/₂-inch pieces**
- 1/2 **pound shrimp**

1. In 3-quart casserole dish, combine onion, oil and garlic. Heat, covered with glass lid, at HIGH 3 to 4 minutes. Add clams, tomatoes, clam juice, bay leaves, salt, pepper, thyme and saffron; heat, covered at HIGH 8 to 10 minutes and on DEFROST 18 to 22 minutes, or until clams are open; stir once.
2. Add scallops, fillet and shrimp. Heat, covered, at HIGH 8 to 10 minutes, or until fish is done.
3. Let stand, covered, 10 minutes before serving.

Memo

Pictured on the following page: Country Ham Casserole ▶

EGGPLANT PARMESAN

Approx. Cooking Time: 26 min.
Yield: 4 servings

- 1 **medium eggplant (about 1³/₄ lbs.)**
- 1 **slice white bread, crumbled**
- ¹/₄ **cup grated Parmesan cheese**
- 2 **tablespoons butter or margarine, melted**
- 2 **cups spaghetti sauce**
- 1¹/₂ **to 2 cups shredded Mozzarella cheese**

1. Pierce skin of eggplant several times; arrange eggplant on paper towel on glass oven tray. Heat 6 to 9 minutes until eggplant is almost tender; let cool, then peel, if desired, and slice into ¹/₂-inch pieces.
2. Meanwhile, combine bread, Parmesan cheese and butter. In 1¹/₂-quart casserole dish, alternately layer spaghetti sauce, eggplant, crumb mixture and mozzarella cheese. Heat for 15 to 17 minutes, giving dish a ¹/₂ turn after 8 minutes.
3. Let stand, covered, 5 minutes before servng.

COUNTRY HAM CASSEROLE

Approx. Cooking Time: 19 min.
Yield: 3 servings

- 1 **package (8 oz.) noodles, cooked and drained**
- 2 **cups cut-up cooked ham (about ¹/₂ lb.)**
- 1¹/₂ **cups shredded Swiss cheese (about 6 oz.)**
- 1 **can (10³/₄ oz.) condensed cream of celery soup**
- 1 **can (8 oz.) green peas, drained**
- ³/₄ **cup milk**
- ¹/₂ **teaspoon dry mustard powder (optional)**
  French fried onion pieces or crushed corn chips

1. In 3-quart casserole dish, combine noodles, ham, 1¹/₄ cups cheese, soup, peas, milk and mustard. Heat, covered, 7 to 8 minutes,stirring once.
2. Top with remaining cheese and onion. Heat 10 to 11 minutes, giving dish ¹/₂ turn after 5 minutes.
3. Let stand 5 minutes before serving.

TUNA CASSEROLE

Approx. Cooking Time: 14 min.
Yield: 4 servings

- 2 **tablespoons butter or margarine, melted**
- 1 **tablespoon soy sauce**
- 1 **teaspoon garlic powder**
- 1 **can (3 oz.) chow mein noodles**
- 1 **can (10³/₄ oz.) condensed cream of mushroom soup**
- 1 **can (7 oz.) tuna, drained and flaked**
- 1 **cup finely chopped celery**
- ¹/₄ **pound salted cashew nuts**
- 2 **teaspoons dried onion flakes**
- ¹/₄ **cup water**

1. Combine butter, soy sauce, garlic and noodles; toss well and reserve. In 1¹/₂-quart casserole, combine soup, tuna, celery, nuts, onion and water.
2. Heat 11 to 13 minutes until heated through, stirring twice. Top with noodle mixture and heat 1 minute. Let stand, 5 minutes.

MAMA'S ITALIAN SAUSAGE

Approx. Cooking Time: 33 min.
Yield: 6 servings

- 1¹/₂ **pounds Italian sausage links, cut into 1-inch pieces**
- 3 **medium potatoes, peeled and cut into small chunks**
- 1 **clove garlic, finely chopped**
- 3 **medium green peppers, cut into chunks**
- 3 **medium onions, cut into chunks**
- 2 **cans (8 oz. ea.) tomato sauce**
- ¹/₂ **teaspoon salt**
- ¹/₂ **teaspoon ground oregano**
- ¹/₄ **teaspoon pepper**

1. In 3-quart casserole dish, combine sausage, potatoes and garlic; heat, covered, 13 to 16 minutes until sausage is almost cooked, stirring once.
2. Drain; stir in remaining ingredients and heat, covered, 13 to 16 minutes until vegetables are tender, stirring twice. Let stand, covered, 5 minutes before serving.

QUICKIE DINNER

Approx. Cooking Time: 15 min.
Yield: 4 servings

- 1 **can (10¾ oz.) condensed cream of chicken or cream of mushroom soup**
- 1 **cup water**
- 2 **teaspoons soy sauce**
- 1½ **to 2 cups cut-up cooked chicken or turkey**
- 1½ **cups packaged precooked rice**
- 1 **can (8 oz.) green peas, drained**
- 2 **tablespoons chopped pimento**

1. In 2-quart casserole dish, blend soup, water, and soy sauce; stir in remaining ingredients. Heat, covered, 13 to 15 minutes until heated through, stirring twice. Let stand, covered, 5 minutes.
2. Top, if desired, with crushed crackers or buttered bread crumbs.

BOSTON EGGPLANT CASSEROLE

Approx. Cooking Time: 12 min.
Yield: 3 to 4 servings

- ½ **pound lean ground beef**
- 1 **small clove of garlic, crushed**
- 1 **small green pepper, finely chopped**
- 2 **slices bacon, cooked and crumbled (reserve drippings)**
- 1 **small onion, finely chopped**
- 1 **small eggplant, peeled and cut into ½-inch slices**
- ¼ **cup crumbled feta cheese**
- ½ **can (15 oz.) tomato sauce**
- ½ **teaspoon salt**
  Pepper to taste
- ½ **cup seasoned croutons**

1. Combine beef, onion, garlic, green pepper and reserved bacon drippings in a medium casserole dish. Heat for 3 to 4 minutes uncovered. Vegetables should be tender and beef slightly browned.
2. Add eggplant slices, feta cheese, tomato sauce, crumbled bacon, salt and pepper. Blend well. Cover and heat for 4 to 6 minutes until eggplant is tender.
3. Sprinkle with croutons and heat an additional ½ to 1 minute until heated through.

SOUTH OF THE BORDER CHILI PIE

Approx. Cooking Time: 19 min.
Yield: 4 to 6 servings

- 1½ **pound lean ground beef**
- 1 **large onion, thinly sliced**
- 1 **can (12 oz.) whole kernel corn, drained**
- 1 **can (16 oz.) whole peeled tomatoes, undrained**
- 1 **can (8 oz.) tomato sauce with cheese**
- 2 **teaspoons chili powder**
- 1 **teaspoon salt**
  Pepper to taste
- ½ **cup shredded Cheddar cheese**
- ⅓ **cup stuffed green olives**
- 1½ **cups coarsely crumbled tortilla chips or corn chips**

1. Crumble beef into a 2-quart casserole dish and add onions. Heat for 7 to 9 minutes until beef is browned. Stir occasionally. Drain.
2. Add corn, tomatoes, tomato sauce, chili powder, salt and pepper. Blend well. Heat, uncovered, for 4 to 5 minutes. Stir occasionally.
3. Arrange olives on top of meat and sprinkle with cheese. Heat, uncovered, for 4 to 5 minutes until cheese begins to melt.
4. Sprinkle with tortilla chips.

HOT TORTILLA DOGS

Approx. Cooking Time: 11 min.
Yield: 4 servings

- 1 **can (16 oz.) chili without beans**
- 3 **tablespoon finely chopped green chili peppers**
- 1/8 **teaspoon hot pepper sauce**
- 8 **tortillas, softened***
- 8 **frankfurters**
- 1 **can (8 oz.) tomato sauce**
- 1 **cup shredded Cheddar cheese**

1. Combine chili, chili peppers and hot pepper sauce. Place 2 tablespoons chili mixture on each tortilla; place frankfurters in center and roll up. In 10 x 6 x 2-inch baking dish, arrange tortillas seamside down.
2. Combine tomato sauce with remaining chili mixture; pour over tortillas. Heat, covered, 9 to 11 minutes until heated through.
3. Top with cheese; let stand, covered, 5 minutes before serving.

***Hint:** *To soften tortillas in your microwave oven, in oblong baking dish, arrange tortillas between layers of damp paper towels. Heat, covered, for 6 to 8 minutes, eight tortillas will soften.*

CORNED BEEF AND CABBAGE

Approx. Cooking Time: 29 min.
Yield: 4 servings

- 2 **medium potatoes, thinly sliced (about 2 cups)**
- 1 **medium onion, sliced**
- 1/4 **cup water**
- 3/4 **teaspoon salt**
- 1/8 **teaspoon pepper**
- 1 **can (12 oz.) corned beef, crumbled**
- 1/2 **head cabbage, cut into 4 wedges (about 1 1/4 lbs.)**
- 1/4 **cup butter or margarine, melted**

1. In greased 3-quart casserole dish, layer potatoes and onion; add water, salt and pepper. Heat, covered, 10 to 12 minutes.

2. Add corned beef and cabbage; pour butter over cabbage. Heat, covered, 15 to 17 minutes until cabbage is tender, giving dish 1/4 turn every 5 minutes. Let stand, covered, 7 minutes before serving.

HAMBURGER TREATS

Approx. Cooking Time: 32 to 34 min.
Yield: 6 servings

- 1 **pound ground beef**
- 1/2 **cup chopped green pepper or onion**
- 1 1/2 **cups water**
- 1 **can (15 oz.) tomato sauce**
- 1 **can (8 oz.) whole kernel corn, undrained**
- 1/2 **8 ounce package elbow macaroni**
- 1/8 **teaspoon hot pepper sauce**
- 1 **cup corn chips, crushed**

1. In 3-quart casserole dish, crumble ground beef; stir in green pepper. Heat 6 to 8 minutes until beef is browned, stirring after 4 minutes. Drain.
2. Stir in water, tomato sauce, corn, macaroni and hot pepper sauce. Heat, covered, 22 to 25 minutes, stirring after 10 minutes.
3. Let stand, covered, 10 minutes; top with corn chips and serve.

Pictured on the following page: Eggs Benedict, Swiss Cheese Fondue, French Omelet ▶

ONION CHEESE PIE

Approx. Cooking Time: 10 min.
Yield: 6 servings

> 3 **eggs, beaten**
> 1 **cup shredded Swiss cheese**
> 1/2 **cup light cream**
> 3 **drops hot pepper sauce**
> 8-**inch pastry crust, baked**
> 1 **can (3 oz.)French fried onions,**
> **chopped**
> **Parsley flakes**

1. Combine eggs, cheese, cream and pepper sauce; pour into prepared crust.
2. Top with onions and parsley. Heat 8 to 10 minutes until center is almost set, giving dish 1/4 turn every 3 minutes. Let stand, covered, 5 minutes before serving.

SPINACH CHEESE RING

Approx. Cooking Time: 11 to 15 min.
Yield: 4 to 6 servings

> 2 **packages (10 oz. ea.) frozen**
> **chopped spinach, cooked and**
> **well drained**
> 1 **cup (1/2 pt.) cottage cheese**
> 2 **eggs, beaten**
> 3 **tablespoons Parmesan cheese**
> 1/2 **teaspoon caraway seeds**
> 1/2 **teaspoon salt**
> **Dash pepper**

1. Thoroughly combine spinach, cottage cheese, eggs, Parmesan cheese, caraway, salt and pepper.
2. Spoon into 9-inch glass pie plate with small glass inverted in center. Heat, covered, 11 to 15 minutes until almost set, giving dish 1/4 turn every 3 minutes.
3. Let stand, covered, 5 minutes before serving.

MACARONI AND CHEESE

Approx. Cooking Time: 13 min.
Yield: 4 servings

> 1 **package (8 oz.) elbow macaroni,**
> **cooked and drained**
> 3/4 **pound pasteurized process**
> **cheese spread, cut into cubes**
> 3/4 **to 1 cup milk**
> 1/2 **to 3/4 teaspoon salt**
> 1/4 **teaspoon onion powder**
> 1/8 **teaspoon dry mustard powder**
> **(optional)**
> 1/4 **teaspoon pepper**
> **Buttered bread crumbs**

1. In 3-quart casserole dish, combine macaroni, cheese, milk, salt, onion powder, mustard and pepper. Heat, covered, 9 to 10 minutes, stirring twice.
2. Top with bread crumbs and heat, uncovered, 3 minutes.

Variation: *Use 1/2 cup tomato sauce for 1/4 cup milk and 1/8 teaspoon oregano for dry mustard.*

SHRIMP FONDUE

Approx. Cooking Time: 8 min.
Yield: 4 servings

> 1 **can (103/4 oz.) condensed cream**
> **of shrimp soup**
> 1 **cup shredded Swiss cheese**
> 1/4 **cup white wine**
> 1/2 **teaspoon Worcestershire sauce**
> **French bread, cut into 1-inch**
> **cubes or bread sticks**

1. In 1-quart casserole dish, combine soup, cheese, wine and Worcestershire sauce.
2. Heat 7 to 8 minutes until cheese is melted, stirring every 2 minutes. Serve hot with French bread.

Pictured on the following page: Home made Gravy, Mornay Sauce, Special Spaghetti Sauce, ▶ Brandied Cherry Sauce, Creamy Salad Dressing

Sauces and Toppings

CRANBERRY SAUCE

Approx. Cooking Time: 15 min.
Yield: 3½ cups

- **2 cups sugar**
- **¼ cup water**
- **1 pound fresh cranberries**
- **1 medium orange**

1. In large glass bowl, combine sugar and water; heat 4 to 6 minutes until sugar is dissolved, stirring once.
2. Add cranberries and heat, covered, 7 to 9 minutes until berries are soft. Meanwhile, grate peel from orange and squeeze juice. Add peel and juice to cranberries.
3. Mash berries with masher or stir well to crush; cool slightly. If desired, add additional sugar to taste; chill before serving.

BORDELAISE SAUCE

Approx. Cooking Time: 12 min.
Yield: 1 cup

- **2 tablespoons finely chopped onion**
- **1 tablespoon butter or margarine**
- **½ cup red wine**
- **1 bay leaf**
- **2 teaspoons cornstarch**
- **½ cup beef broth**
- **1 teaspoon butter**
- **1 teaspoon parsley flakes**

1. In 2-cup measure heat onion and butter 1 to 2 minutes, add wine and bay leaf. Heat 5 to 6 minutes until mixture is reduced to ⅓ cup.
2. Strain. Into wine mixture stir cornstarch blended with broth and heat 3 to 4 minutes until sauce is thickened, stirring once. Stir in butter and parsley.

Variation: *With broth, add 1 can (2 oz.) sliced mushrooms, drained.*

HOMEMADE GRAVY

Approx. Cooking Time: 7 min.
Yield: 1 cup

- **1 to 2 tablespoons butter or margarine**
- **2 tablespoons flour**
  Salt and pepper to taste
  Few drops browning sauce (optional)
- **1 cup roast drippings***

1. In small glass bowl, heat butter 1 minute until melted; stir in flour, salt, pepper and browning sauce.
2. Gradually add drippings, stirring until smooth; heat 3 to 5 minutes until gravy is thickened, stirring twice.

* *If necessary, add broth, milk or water to roast drippings to equal 1 cup. If using milk, heat for 3 to 4 minutes.*

BASIC WHITE SAUCE

Approx. Cooking Time: 7 min.
Yield: 1 cup

- **2 tablespoons butter or margarine**
- **2 tablespoons flour**
- **½ teaspoon salt (optional)**
- **1 cup milk**

1. In small glass bowl, heat butter 1 minute until melted; stir in flour and salt.
2. Gradually add milk, stirring until smooth. Heat 5 to 6 minutes until sauce is thickened, stirring occasionally.

Variations:
For CHEESE Sauce, *Stir in ½ to ¾ cup shredded cheese. Heat 1 minute, if necessary, to completely melt cheese.*
For CURRY Sauce, *stir in 1 to 2 teaspoons curry powder.*
For HORSERADISH Sauce, *add 1 tablespoon prepared horseradish.*
For MUSTARD Sauce, *add 2 tablespoons prepared mustard and dash Worcestershire sauce.*

CREAMY SALAD DRESSING

Approx. Cooking Time: 5 min.
Yield: 1 cup

- 1/2 **cup water**
- 1/3 **cup vinegar**
- 1/4 **to** 1/3 **cup sugar**
- 1 **egg**
- 1 **tablespoon flour**
- 1 **teaspoon salt**
- 1/2 **teaspoon dry mustard**
- 1 **tablespoon butter or margarine**

1. In medium glass bowl, with wire whip or rotary beater, thoroughly combine water, vinegar, sugar, egg, flour, salt and mustard. Heat 4 to 5 minutes until mixture is thickened, stirring twice; stir in butter.
2. Use in place of mayonnaise when making coleslaw or potato salad.

MORNAY SAUCE

Approx. Cooking Time: 10 min.
Yield: 1½ cups

- 2 **tablespoons butter or margarine**
- 2 **tablespoons flour**
- 1 **cup chicken broth**
- 1/3 **cup light cream or milk**
- 1/4 **cup shredded Swiss cheese**
- 1/4 **cup Parmesan cheese**
- 2 **tablespoons parsley flakes**

1. In small glass bowl, heat butter 1 minute until melted; stir in flour.
2. Gradually add broth and cream, stirring until smooth. Heat 5 to 6 minutes until sauce is slightly thickened, stirring twice.
3. Stir in cheese and parsley. Heat 3 to 4 minutes until cheese is melted, stirring twice.

CARAMEL SAUCE

Approx. Cooking Time: 6 min.
Yield: 1¼ cups

- 1/4 **teaspoon ground cinnamon**
- 1 **package (14 oz.) caramels**
- 2 **tablespoons rum (optional)**
- 1 **tablespoon water**

1. In small bowl, combine all ingredients.
2. Heat 4 to 6 minutes, stirring twice, until smooth.

SWEET AND SOUR SAUCE

Approx. Cooking Time: 8 min.
Yield: 2 cups

- **Water**
- 1 **can (8**1/4 **oz.) crushed pineapple in heavy syrup, drained (reserve syrup)**
- 1/4 **cup brown sugar**
- 1 **tablespoon soy sauce (optional)**
- 1 **tablespoon cornstarch**
- 1/3 **to** 1/2 **cup cider vinegar**

1. In 2-cup glass measure, add enough water to reserved syrup to equal 3/4 cup; stir in pineapple, brown sugar and soy sauce. Heat 3 to 4 minutes, stirring once.
2. Stir in cornstarch blended with vinegar; heat 3 to 4 minutes until sauce is slightly thickened, stirring once.

Variation: *Add ½ cup finely chopped green pepper with pineapple.*

RAISIN SAUCE

Approx. Cooking Time: 8 min.
Yield: 1½ cups

- 1/2 **cup orange juice**
- 1/2 **cup raisins**
- 1/3 **cup currant jelly** *
- **Dash ground allspice**
- 1 **tablespoon rum (optional)**
- 1 **tablespoon cornstarch**
- 1/2 **cup water**

1. In small glass bowl, heat orange juice, raisins, jelly and allspice 2 to 3 minutes, stirring once.
2. Add rum and cornstarch blended with water. Heat 4 to 5 minutes until sauce is thickened, stirring occasionally.

*Substitution: *Use pineapple or apricot preserves for currant jelly.*

BRANDIED CHERRY SAUCE

Approx. Cooking Time: 12 min.
Yield: 6 servings

1 can (17 oz.) dark sweet pitted cherries in heavy syrup, drained (reserve syrup)
Water
1/2 cup sugar
1 1/2 tablespoons cornstarch
1/4 cup brandy

1. Reserve 1/4 cup syrup. To remaining syrup, add enough water to equal 1 1/4 cups. In medium glass bowl, combine syrup-water mixture, cherries and sugar; heat 4 to 6 minutes, stirring once.
2. Stir in cornstarch blended with reserved syrup and heat 3 to 4 minutes until sauce is thickened, stirring once. Transfer to serving dish.
3. In 1-cup glass measure, heat brandy 1 minute. Pour over cherries and carefully flame. Serve, over vanilla ice cream, angel food cake or chocolate souffle.

BANANA SPLIT TOPPING

Approx. Cooking Time: 10 min.
Yield: 3 cups

1 can (8 1/4 oz.) pineapple chunks, drained (reserve syrup)
1 can (17 oz.) dark sweet pitted cherries in heavy syrup, drained (reserve syrup)
1 1/2 tablespoons cornstarch
2 bananas, cut into 1-inch pieces

1. Reserve 1/4 cup syrup. In medium glass bowl, combine remaining syrups, pineapple and cherries; heat 4 to 6 minutes, stirring once.
2. Stir in cornstarch blended with reserved syrup and heat 3 to 4 minutes until sauce is thickened, stirring once.
3. Cool slightly; slice bananas over ice cream and add topping.

SPICY PINEAPPLE SAUCE

Approx. Cooking Time: 10 min.
Yield: 3/4 cup

2 tablespoons sugar
1 tablespoon cornstarch
1 can (8 oz.) unsweetened pineapple chunks with juice
1/4 teaspoon cinnamon
2 tablespoons butter or margarine

1. Combine sugar and cornstarch in a small casserole dish. Gradually add juice from pineapple, stirring constantly. Add pineapple, cinnamon and butter. Stir.
2. Heat for 4 to 5 minutes, uncovered.
3. Stir and continue cooking an additional 4 to 6 minutes until sauce is thickened. Stir occasionally. Serve over pork, poultry or as a dessert topping.

ORANGE GLAZE

Approx. Cooking Time: 2 min.
Yield: 1 cup

1/2 cup honey
2/3 cup orange marmalade

1. Combine ingredients in a small glass bowl and heat, uncovered, 1 to 2 minutes until glaze is hot.
2. Use as a glaze on ham or poultry.

MELBA SAUCE

Approx. Cooking Time: 7 min.
Yield: 2 cups

1 package (10 oz.) frozen raspberries in heavy syrup, thawed
1 can (8 1/4 oz.) sliced peaches, drained (reserve syrup)
1/4 cup water
1 1/2 tablespoons cornstarch

1. In small glass bowl, combine raspberries, reserved syrup, water and cornstarch. Heat 6 to 6 1/2 minutes until sauce is thickened, stirring once. Chill.
2. Before serving, add peaches. Serve, over pound cake, ice cream or shortcake.

VANILLA SAUCE

Approx. Cooking Time: 7 min.
Yield: 1½ cups

- **1 cup milk**
- **⅓ cup sugar**
- **1½ tablespoons cornstarch**
- **1 tablespoon butter or margarine**
- **1 teaspoon vanilla extract**

1. In medium glass bowl, heat ¾ cup milk and sugar 3 to 4 minutes until sugar is dissolved, stirring once.
2. Stir in cornstarch blended with remaining milk and heat 2 to 3 minutes until sauce is thickened, stirring once. Stir in butter and vanilla; chill. Serve in place of whipped cream.

LEMON SAUCE

Approx. Cooking Time: 8 min.
Yield: 1 cup

- **1 cup water**
- **⅓ cup sugar**
- **1 tablespoon cornstarch**
- **1 tablespoon lemon juice**
- **1 tablespoon butter or margarine**
- **1 drop yellow food coloring**

1. In medium glass bowl, heat ¾ cup water and sugar 3 to 4 minutes until sugar is dissolved, stirring once.
2. Stir in cornstarch blended with remaining water and lemon juice; heat 3 to 4 minutes until sauce is thickened, stirring once.
3. Stir in butter and food coloring; cool slightly before serving.

ORANGE LIQUEUR SAUCE

Approx. Cooking Time: 3 min.
Yield: 1 cup

- **½ cup water**
- **¼ cup orange juice**
- **3 to 4 tablespoons sugar**
- **1 tablespoon cornstarch**
- **1 to 2 tablespoons orange flavored liqueur**

1. In small glass bowl, combine water, orange juice, sugar and cornstarch. Heat 2 to 3 minutes until sauce is thickened, stirring once; stir in liqueur.
2. Serve, over rice pudding, chocolate mousse or plain cake.

NEWBURG SAUCE

Power Level: HIGH
                DEFROST
Approx. Cooking Time: 11 min.
Yield: 2½ cups

- **1 cup half and half or light cream**
- **1 cup milk**
- **3 to 4 tablespoons sherry**
- **3 tablespoons flour**
- **3 egg yolks**
- **Salt and pepper to taste**

1. In medium glass bowl, combine cream, milk, sherry and flour. Heat 7 to 9 minutes on HIGH until sauce is slightly thickened, stirring twice. With wire whip, quickly stir in egg yolks; season with salt and pepper.
2. Heat 1 to 2 minutes on DEFROST until sauce is thickened, stirring twice.

HOLLANDAISE SAUCE

Power Level: HIGH
                DEFROST
Approx Cooking Time: 6 min.
Yield: 1½ cups

- **3 tablespoons butter or margarine**
- **2 tablespoons flour**
- **1 cup hot water**
- **1 to 2 tablespoons lemon juice**
- **2 egg yolks**
- **Salt and pepper to taste**

1. In small glass bowl, heat butter 1 to 1½ minutes on HIGH until melted; stir in flour; gradually add water and lemon juice. Heat 2 to 3 minutes on HIGH until sauce is slightly thickened, stirring once. Quickly add egg yolks, stirring constantly with wire whip.
2. Heat 1 to 2 minutes on DEFROST until sauce is thickened, stirring once. Season with salt and pepper.

CREOLE SAUCE

Power Level: HIGH
            DEFROST
Approx. Cooking Time: 9 min. .
Yield: 2½ cups

¼ cup finely chopped onion
¼ cup finely chopped green pepper
¼ cup thinly sliced celery
2 tablespoons butter or margarine
1 teaspoon finely chopped garlic
¼ to ½ teaspoon chili powder
1 can (15 oz.) tomato sauce

1. In medium glass bowl, combine onion, green pepper, celery, butter, garlic and chili powder; heat, covered, 3 to 5 minutes on HIGH. Stir in tomato sauce.
2. Continue cooking on DEFROST an additonal 3 to 4 minutes, stirring once.

BARBECUE SAUCE

Power Level: HIGH
            DEFROST
Approx. Cooking Time: 15 min.
Yield: 2 cups

1 cup chili sauce
¾ cup water
¼ cup lemon juice
1 envelope (1¾ oz.) onion soup mix
½ cup brown sugar
1 teaspoon dry mustard
⅛ teaspoon garlic powder

1. In medium glass bowl, combine all ingredients; heat 7 minutes on HIGH, stirring once.
2. Continue cooking on DEFROST an additional 6 to 8 minutes until sauce is slightly thickened, stirring twice. Use as a basting sauce on chicken, ribs, hamburgers.

BEARNAISE SAUCE

Power Level: HIGH
            DEFROST
Approx. Cooking Time: 6 min.
Yield: ½ cup

¼ cup finely chopped onion
2 tablespoons wine vinegar

4 egg yolks
¼ cup butter or margarine
1 teaspoon parsley flakes

1. In small glass bowl, heat onion and vinegar 2 to 3 minutes on HIGH. Stir in egg yolks until well blended.
2. Heat 1 to 2 minutes on DEFROST until sauce is thickened, stirring twice; stir in butter until melted. Heat 1 minute on DEFROST, strring once. Strain and sprinkle with parsley.

CUSTARD SAUCE

Power Level: HIGH
            DEFROST
Approx. Cooking Time: 8 min.
Yield: 2 cups

3 tablespoons sugar
2 tablespoons flour
1½ cups milk
2 egg yolks, beaten
1 teaspoon vanilla extract

1. In 1-qt. glass measuring cup, combine sugar and flour; gradually stir in milk. Heat 5 to 6 minutes on HIGH until sauce is slightly thickened, stirring every 2 minutes.
2. With wire whip, quickly stir in egg yolks.
3. Heat 1 to 2 minutes on DEFROST until sauce is thickened, stirring after 1 minute. Stir in vanilla. Chill slightly before serving.

QUICK SPAGHETTI SAUCE

Power Level: HIGH
            DEFROST
Approx. Cooking Time: 11 min.
Yield: 2½ cups

½ cup finely chopped onion
2 tablespoons oil
2 teaspoons finely chopped garlic
1 teaspoon oregano
⅛ teaspoon basil
2 teaspoons sugar (optional)
2 cans (8 oz. ea.) tomato sauce

1. In medium glass bowl, combine onion, oil, garlic, oregano and basil. Heat, covered, 3 to 3½ minutes on HIGH until onion is tender, stirring once.
2. Stir in remaining ingredients and heat 3 to 4 minutes on HIGH.
3. Continue cooking on DEFROST an additional 3 to 4 minutes, stirring once.

CREAMY CORN CHOWDER

Approx. Cooking Time: 16 min.
Yield: 4 servings

- **3 tablespoons butter or margarine**
- **1/4 cup finely chopped celery**
- **3 tablespoons flour**
- **1 teaspoon dried chives or dried onion flakes**
- **1 teaspoon salt**
- **1/8 teaspoon pepper**
- **2 cups milk**
- **1 can (17 oz.) cream-style corn**

1. In 2-quart casserole dish, heat butter and celery 2 to 3 minutes. Stir in flour, chives, salt and pepper; gradually add milk stirring until smooth. Heat 5 1/2 to 7 1/2 minutes until soup is slightly thickened, stirring twice.
2. Add corn and heat 4 to 5 minutes until heated through, stirring twice. Let stand, covered, 3 minutes before serving.

VEGETABLE BEEF SOUP

Approx. Cooking Time: 25 to 29 min.
Yield: 4 to 5 servings

- **1/2 pound ground beef**
- **2 1/2 cups water**
- **1 can (16 oz.) stewed tomatoes**
- **1/2 cup potatoes, diced**
- **1/4 cup celery, diced**
- **1/4 cup onion, diced**
- **1 package (10 oz.) frozen mixed vegetables, thawed**
- **1 teaspoon parsley flakes**
- **1 teaspoon salt**
- **1/8 teaspoon pepper**

1. In 3-quart casserole dish, crumble ground beef and heat for 3 to 4 minutes, stirring after 2 minutes. Drain.
2. Add remaining ingredients and mix thoroughly.
3. Cover and heat 22 to 25 minutes, stirring occasionally.

EVERYDAY SUPPER SOUPS

Approx. Cooking Time: 15 min.
Yield: 6 servings each

Cheesy Tomato Soup:

- **1 can (11 oz.) condensed Cheddar cheese soup**
- **1 can (10 3/4 oz.) condensed tomato soup**
- **2 cans water**
- **1/4 teaspoon basil**

1. In a 2-quart casserole, combine all ingredients; heat 12 to 15 minutes until heated through, stirring occasionally. Let stand, covered, 5 minutes before serving.
2. Garnish, with seasoned croutons or small pretzel rings.

Creamy Noodle Soup:

- **1 can (10 3/4 oz.) condensed turkey noodle soup**
- **1 can (10 3/4 oz.) condensed cream of mushroom soup**
- **1 1/2 cans water**
- **1/8 teaspoon sage**

1. Follow above procedure for Cheesy Tomato Soup.
2. Garnish, if desired, with toasted slivered almonds.

PAWTUCKET CLAM CHOWDER

Approx. Cooking time: 15 min.
Yield: 4 servings

- **1 can (10 1/2 oz.) condensed vegetable soup**
- **1 1/2 cups tomato juice**
- **1 can (7 1/2 oz.) minced clams**
  Dash thyme

1. In 1 1/2-quart casserole dish, combine all ingredients; heat, covered, 12 to 15 minutes until heated through, stirring occasionally.
2. Let stand, covered, 5 minutes.

CURRY SOUP

Approx. Cooking Time: 13 min.
Yield: 6 servings

- **1 can (11 oz.) condensed tomato bisque soup**
- **1 can (10³/4 oz.) condensed cream of chicken soup**
- **1/4 cup flaked coconut or unsalted peanuts**
- **1 to 2 teaspoons curry powder**
- **3 cups milk**
- **1/2 cup chopped apple***

1. In 2-quart casserole dish, combine all ingredients.
2. Heat, covered, 12 to 13 minutes until heated through, stirring once. Let stand, covered, 5 minutes before serving.

***Variation:** *Use 2 tablespoons sliced green onion for apple.*

OLD FASHIONED RUSSIAN BORSCHT

Approx. Cooking Time: 13 min.
Yield: 2 servings

- **1/2 cup onion, finely chopped**
- **2 tablespoons butter or margarine**
- **1 can (16 oz.) diced red beets, drained**
- **2 cups hot water**
- **1 tablespoon instant beef bouillon**
- **1/2 teaspoon salt**
  Dash of Tabasco sauce
- **1 tablespoon lemon juice**
  Dairy sour cream

1. Combine onion and butter in a 2-quart casserole and heat for 3 to 5 minutes until onion is tender.
2. Place beets and onion mixture in an electric blender and blend until smooth. Mix beet mixture with water, beef bouillon, salt and Tabasco sauce, and heat for 6 to 8 minutes.
3. Stir in lemon juice and serve in individual serving, bowls; add sour cream as desired.

LENTIL-HAM SOUP

Approx. Cooking Time: 30 min.
Yield: 4 to 5 servings

- **3/4 cup lentils**
- **1¹/2 quarts of water**
- **1 cup cooked ham, diced**
- **1/2 teaspoon browning sauce**
- **1 teaspoon salt**
- **1/4 teaspoon pepper**
- **1/4 teaspoon oregano**
- **1/4 cup onion, chopped**
- **1/4 cup carrot, thinly sliced**
- **1/4 cup celery, thinly sliced**
- **1 tablespoon parsley flakes**
- **1/2 cup potatoes, peeled and diced**

1. Soak lentils in 2 cups of water overnight in refrigerator. Drain and combine with remaining ingredients in a 2-quart casserole.
2. Cover and heat for 27 to 30 minutes until vegetables are tender. Stir occasionally.

ZUCCHINI SOUP

Approx. Cooking Time: 18 min.
Yield: 2 servings

- **1¹/2 small zucchini cut into 1-inch chunks (about 1¹/2 cups)**
- **1/3 cup condensed consommé**
- **3/4 cup water**
- **1 slice bacon, cooked crisp and crumbled**
- **2 tablespoons onion, chopped**
- **1/4 teaspoon seasoned salt**
- **1/4 teaspoon salt**
- **1/4 teaspoon basil**
- **1/4 teaspoon garlic powder**
- **1 tablespoon fresh parsley, chopped**
  Pepper to taste
  Parmesan cheese, grated

1. Combine all ingredients, except Parmesan cheese in a 1-quart casserole. Cover and heat for 10 to 13 minutes until zucchini is tender. Stir once. Cool.
2. Process soup in an electric blender until smooth. Return to casserole, heat for 3 to 4 minutes.
3. Serve in individual soup bowls, sprinkling the top with grated Parmesan cheese.

DUMPLINGS FOR STEW

Approx. Cooking Time: 9 min.
Yield: 4 to 6 servings
   4   to 6 servings cooked stew
   2   cups buttermilk biscuit mix
   2/3   cup milk

1. Bring stew ingredients to a boil.
2. Combine biscuit mix and milk until
   smooth; drop by tablespoonfuls around
   edge of stew, forming about 10 dumplings. Heat, covered, 6 to 9 minutes
   until dumplings are cooked.

GERMAN STEW

Power Level: HIGH—DEFROST—HIGH
Approx. Cooking Time: 56 min.
Yield: 6 servings

1 1/2   pounds beef cut into strips
   2   cups water
   2   medium onions, sliced
   1/4   cup cider vinegar
   1   tablespoon sugar
   1   bay leaf
   1   teaspoon salt
   1/2   teaspoon caraway seeds
   **1   small head (about 1 lb.) red
        cabbage, shredded***
   1/4   cup flour

1. In 3-quart casserole dish, combine beef,
   1 1/2 cups water, onions, vinegar, sugar,
   bay leaf, salt and caraway. Heat, covered,
   9 to 11 minutes on HIGH.
2. Continue cooking on DEFROST an
   additional 13 to 15 minutes, stirring occasionally.
3. Add red cabbage and heat, covered, 17
   to 22 minutes on HIGH until beef and
   cabbage are tender, stirring occasionally.
4. Stir in flour blended with remaining water
   and heat 6 to 8 minutes on HIGH until
   stew is thickened, stirring once.

*Substitution: *Use 1 jar (16 oz.) red
                    cabbage, drained for
                    fresh red cabbage.*

BEER STEW

Power Level: HIGH
                DEFROST
Approx. Cooking Time: 35 min.
Yield: 6 servings

**1 1/2   pounds beef, cut into 1-inch
        pieces**
   1   cup beef broth
   1/2   cup beer
   1   tablespoon brown sugar
1 1/2   teaspoons salt
   1/2   teaspoon pepper
   1/2   teaspoon caraway seeds
   **1   cup sliced onions (about 3
        small)**
   1   package (10 oz.) frozen peas
   3   tablespoons flour
   1/4   cup water
   1   regular size cooking bag

1. Place cooking bag in 2-quart casserole
   dish. Combine beef, broth, beer, sugar,
   salt, pepper and caraway in bag, turning
   bag several times to mix. Pull bag up
   around beef and tie. Make six half-inch
   slits in top of bag. Heat 8 to 11 minutes
   on HIGH.
2. Continue cooking on DEFROST an
   additional 8 to 10 minutes. Add onions
   and peas; reclose. Heat an additional 13
   minutes on DEFROST until beef and
   vegetables are tender. Carefully open
   bag and turn down sides.
3. Stir in flour blended with water and heat
   1 minute on DEFROST until slightly thickened.

*Pictured on the following page: Spanish Rice, Macaroni and Cheese Dinner, Citrus Style ▶
Noodles, Brown Rice*

Pastas,Grains and Cereals

PREPARING PASTA

- Combine pasta, very hot water and salt in recommended cooking dish.
- Heat, covered, stirring after 10 minutes.
- Test pasta for desired doneness before adding more cooking time.

- Slightly undercook pasta that will be heated again in casseroles.
- Stir and let stand, covered, 5 minutes.
- Drain and rinse before serving.

ITEM	CONTAINER	HOT WATER	COOK TIME (in min.)
Egg Noodles, medium width (8 oz.)	3-qt. casserole dish	6 cups	17 to 19
Elbow Macaroni (8 oz.)	2-qt. casserole dish	3 cups	18 to 20
Spaghetti (8 oz.-broken)	3-qt. casserole dish	6 cups	20 to 22
Specialty Noodles (Bows, shells etc, 8 oz.)	2-qt. casserole dish	3 cups	18 to 20

CITRUS STYLE NOODLES

Approx. Cooking Time: 24 min.
Yield: 4 servings

> 1 **package (8 oz.) medium egg noodles**
> 1/2 **cup almonds**
> 1/4 **cup butter or margarine**
> 1 **tablespoon poppy seeds**
> 1 1/2 **teaspoons grated lemon peel**
> 1 1/2 **teaspoons grated orange peel**
> 1/2 **teaspoon salt**
> 1/8 **teaspoon pepper**
> 1 **cup sour cream**

1. Cook noodles, according to chart.
2. While noodles are standing, in glass serving bowl, heat almonds and butter 1 1/2 to 2 minutes until butter is melted.
3. Stir in drained noodles, poppy seeds, lemon and orange peel, salt and pepper, toss well. Serve with sour cream.

PARMESAN NOODLES

Approx. Cooking Time: 25 min.
Yield: 4 servings

> 1 **package (8 oz.) medium egg noodles**
> 1 **cup grated Parmesan cheese**
> 1/2 **cup butter or margarine, cut into quarters**
> 1/2 **cup heavy cream**
> **Pepper to taste**

1. Cook noodles, according to chart.
2. While noodles are standing, in glass serving bowl, heat cheese, butter and cream 4 to 5 minutes until butter is melted, stirring twice.
3. Stir in drained noodles; toss well. Season with pepper.

PREPARING RICE AND OTHER GRAINS

- Combine rice or other grains, very hot water and salt in recommended cooking dish.
- Heat, covered, stirring after half of cooking time.

  Let stand, covered, 5 minutes before serving.

Note: **For instant (no cook) products,** *using package directions, bring hot water to a boil. Stir in product; let stand, covered.*

RICE COOKING CHART

ITEM	CONTAINER		RICE	COOK TIME (in min)
Long Grain Rice	2 qt.	2¼ cups, 1 tsp. salt	1 cup	18 to 20
Short Grain Rice	2 qt.	2¼ cups, 1 tsp. salt	1 cup	18 to 20
Rice Casserole Mix	2 qt.	2 cups, 1 tsp. salt	6 oz. pkg.	15 to 17
Quick Cooking Rice	1½ qt.	1 cup, 1 tsp. salt	1 cup	4 to 5
Brown Rice	2 qt. Covered Glass Bowl	1 cup, 1 tsp. salt	1 cup	25
Cereal Barley	2 qt. Covered Glass Bowl	4 cups, 1 tsp. salt	1 cup	25

POPEYE RICE

Approx. Cooking Time: 20 min.
Yield: 4 to 6 servings

  2 cups water
  1 cup long grain rice
1¼ cups fresh chopped spinach
 ¼ cup chopped green onion
 ¼ cup chopped celery
  2 tablespoons lemon juice
 ¼ cup chopped parsley
1½ teaspoons salt

1. Place all ingredients in 2-quart casserole.
2. Cover; cook for 18 to 20 minutes or until liquid is almost absorbed, stir 3 times during cooking.
3. Let stand, covered, for 5 minutes or until remaining liquid is absorbed.

SOUTH OF THE BORDER RICE

Approx. Cooking Time: 20 min.
Yield: 4 servings

- **6 slices bacon**
- **3/4 cup water**
- **1 can (16 oz.) whole tomatoes, undrained and chopped**
- **1 packed (6 oz.) Spanish rice mix**
- **6 stuffed green olives, sliced**

1. In 10 x 6 x 2-inch dish, place 3 slices of bacon on 2 layers of paper towels. Cover with paper towel and add remaining 3 slices of bacon. Cover with paper towel and heat 6 to 8 minutes, giving dish 1/4 turn after 3 minutes.
2. Drain and reserve drippings. In glass bowl, combine bacon drippings, water, tomatoes and Spanish rice mix. Cover; cook for 12 minutes or until liquid is almost completely absorbed.
3. Crumble bacon and mix into rice. Garnish with sliced olives.

CHEESY RICE

Approx. Cooking Time: 25 min.
Yield: 4 servings

- **2 cups water**
- **1 cup long grain rice**
- **8 ounces grated Cheddar cheese (about 2 cups)**
- **1 teaspoon salt**
- **1/2 teaspoon garlic powder**
- **2 cups milk**
- **1 tablespoon chopped parsley**
- **1/4 cup grated Parmesan cheese**
- **1/4 cup slivered almonds**
  Salt to taste

1. In 2-quart casserole, combine water, rice, cheese, salt, garlic powder and milk. Cover; cook for 25 minutes or until almost all liquid is absorbed. Stir every 5 minutes.
2. Stir in remaining ingredients.
3. Let stand, covered, for 5 minutes.

GRANOLA

Approx. Cooking Time: 11 min.
Yield: 6 cups

- **2/3 cup raisins**
  Water
- **1/4 cup brown sugar**
- **1/4 cup salad oil**
- **1/4 cup honey**
- **4 cups rolled oats**
- **1/2 cup sliced almonds**
- **1/4 cup wheat germ**
  Dash each cinnamon, cloves, nutmeg, salt

1. Soak raisins in hot water to cover for 10 minutes or until plump; drain.
2. In glass bowl, combine sugar, oil and honey; cook for 1 minute or until sugar is melted, stir well. In larger glass dish, mix together rolled oats, almonds, wheat germ, and spices. Pour sugar mixture over dry ingredients; mix well.
3. Cook for 10 minutes; stirring every two minutes.

MACABEEF

Approx. Cooking Time: 15 min.
Yield: 4 servings

- **1 pound lean ground beef**
- **4 cups cooked macaroni**
- **1 jar (16-ounces) spaghetti sauce**
  Salt to taste

1. In 2-quart casserole, cook beef for 5 minutes or until no longer pink. Drain. Stir in remaining ingredients.
2. Cover; cook for 10 minutes or until hot, stirring after 5 minutes.

CURRIED RICE

Approx. Cooking Time: 4 min.
Yield: 6 servings

- **1/4 cup chopped onion**
- **1/4 cup chopped green pepper**
- **2 tablespoons butter**
- **3 cups hot cooked rice**
- **1/2 teaspoon curry powder**
- **3/4 teaspoon salt**

1. In 1 1/2-quart casserole combine onion, green pepper, and butter. Cook for 2 minutes, or until onion is soft.
2. Add remaining ingredients, mixing well.
3. Cover; cook for 2 minutes to heat through.

CONFETTI RICE

Approx. Cooking Time: 21 min.
Yield: 6 servings

¹/₂ cup chopped onions
¹/₂ cup sliced mushrooms
3 tablespoons butter
2 cups hot water
2 chicken bouillon cubes
1 cup long grain rice
1 package (10-oz.) frozen peas and carrots, defrosted
¹/₂ teaspoon salt
Pepper to taste

1. In 2-quart casserole combine onion, mushrooms and butter. Cook for 3 minutes, or until onions are soft.
2. Add water, bouillon cubes and rice. Cover; cook for 10 minutes, stirring after 5 minutes. Stir in peas and carrots. Cover; cook for 6 to 8 minutes, stirring after 4 minutes.
3. Add salt and pepper before serving.

PREPARING HOT CEREALS

- Combine cereal, hot water* and salt (optional) in dish.
- Heat, stirring once.

- Let stand; stir before serving.
- Top as desired, with sugar, spices, etc.

CEREAL	CONTAINER	HOT WATER	CEREAL	CEREAL COOK TIME (in min.)	STANDING TIME (in min.)
Cream of Wheat*					
1 serving	2 cup glass bowl	1¹/₄ cups	2¹/₂ tablespoons	1¹/₂	2
2 servings	1-qt. glass bowl	2 cups	¹/₃ cup	2	2
4 servings	2-qt. glass bowl	3³/₄ cups	²/₃ cup	3	3
Farina					
1 serving	individual serving dish	²/₃ cup	2 tablespoons	2 to 3	2
2 servings	2 individual serving dishes	1¹/₃ cups	¹/₄ cups	5 to 5¹/₂	2
4 servings	1-qt. glass bowl	2²/₃ cups	¹/₂ cup	6¹/₂ to 8	3
Oatmeal (Quick)					
1 serving	individual serving dish	³/₄ cup	¹/₃ cup	1¹/₂ to 2	2
2 servings	2 individual serving dishes			3 to 3¹/₂	2
4 servings	1-qt. glass bowl	3 cups	1¹/₃ cups	5 to 6	3
Oatmeal (Old-Fashioned)					
1 serving	individual serving dish	³/₄ cup	¹/₃ cup	4 to 5	2
2 servings	2 individual serving dishes	1¹/₂ cups	²/₃ cup	7 to 9	2
4 servings	2-qt. glass bowl	3 cups	1¹/₃ cup	10 to 12	3

* For Cream of Wheat, heat water to boil, then add cereal.

CHUCKWAGON SPECIAL

Power Level: HIGH
DEFROST
Approx. Cooking Time: 26 to 30 min.
Yield: 6 servings

4 slices bacon, diced
1 medium onion, chopped
2¹/₂ cups hot water
1¹/₂ cups cooked black-eyed peas
1 cup long grain rice
1 teaspoon salt
¹/₄ teaspoon pepper
Dash hot pepper sauce
(optional)

1. In 2-quart casserole dish, heat bacon and onion 7 to 8 minutes on HIGH until bacon is crisp, stirring once.
2. Stir in remaining ingredients. Heat, covered, 9 to 10 minutes on HIGH until liquid boils.
3. Continue cooking on DEFROST an additional 10 to 12 minutes until rice is tender, stirring once. Let stand, covered, 5 minutes before serving.

SPANISH RICE

Power Level: HIGH
DEFROST
Approx. Cooking Time: 26 min.
Yield: 6 servings

¹/₂ cup chopped onion
¹/₄ cup finely chopped green pepper
2 tablespoons butter or margarine
Water
1 can (16 oz.) stewed tomatoes, chopped and drained (reserve liquid)
1 cup long grain rice
1¹/₂ teaspoons salt
¹/₈ teaspoon pepper

1. In 2-quart casserole dish, heat onion, green pepper and butter 4 to 6 minutes on HIGH, stirring once.
2. Add enough water to reserved liquid to equal 2 cups. Add to dish with tomatoes, rice, salt and pepper. Heat, covered, 6 to 8 minutes on HIGH.

3. Continue cooking on DEFROST an additional 12 to 14 minutes until rice is tender, stirring once. Let stand, covered, 5 minutes before serving.

RICE DELIGHT

Power Level: HIGH
DEFROST
Approx. Cooking Time: 24 min.
Yield: 6 servings

¹/₄ cup butter or margarine
1 cup long grain rice
2¹/₄ cups chicken broth
¹/₄ cup raisins (optional)
1 to 1¹/₂ teaspoons curry powder

1. In 2-quart casserole, heat butter 1 to 2 minutes on HIGH until melted; stir in rice. Heat 3 to 5 minutes on HIGH until rice is browned, stirring once.
2. Add remaining ingredients and heat, covered, 6 to 8 minutes on HIGH.
3. Continue cooking on DEFROST an additional 10 to 11 minutes until rice is tender. Let stand, covered, 5 minutes.

BARLEY MUSHROOM CASSEROLE

Power Level: HIGH
DEFROST
Approx. Cooking Time: 20 min.
Yield: 6 servings

6 tablespoons butter or margarine
2 medium onions, finely chopped
3 cloves garlic, finely chopped
1 pound fresh mushrooms, sliced
1 cup quick cooking barley
¹/₂ cup chicken broth
¹/₄ cup chopped parsley
2 teaspoons basil
1 teaspoon salt
¹/₄ teaspoon pepper

1. In 2-quart casserole, heat, covered, butter, onion and garlic 4 to 6 minutes on HIGH until onion is tender. Stir in remaining ingredients. Heat, covered, 8 minutes on HIGH.
2. Continue cooking on DEFROST an additional 4 to 6 minutes until barley is tender. Let stand, covered. 5 minutes before serving.

Pictured on the following page: Ratatouille▶

Vegetables and Other Side Meals

SPECIAL HINTS FOR PREPARING FRESH AND FROZEN VEGETABLES

FRESH Vegetables

- Weights given for fresh vegetables are purchase weights, before peeling, trimming etc.
- Pierce skins of vegetables to be heated whole and unpeeled (i.e. eggplant, potatoes, squash). This allows steam to escape and prevents vegetables from popping or bursting. Arrange vegetables on paper towel lined glass oven tray.
- Add only 2 to 3 tablespoons water per pound. Often, rinsing vegetables before cooking is sufficient. Salt just before serving.
- Heat, covered, in casserole dish; stirring once. Heat corn on the cob in oblong baking dish; rearrange once during cooking.
- Let stand, covered, as specified in the chart or recipe.

FROZEN Vegetables

- Frozen vegetables may be heated in pouch, package or freezer container. Puncture pouch before heating, and flex halfway through cooking to distribute heat.
- Place frozen vegetables in covered casserole dish. Add 2 tablespoons of water unless otherwise indicated in chart.
- Stir once during cooking. Arrange corn on the cob in oblong baking dish, rearrange once during cooking.
- Salt vegetables after cooking or put salt in the casserole with the water before adding vegetables.

VEGETABLE	AMT.	COOK TIME (in min.)	STANDING TIME (in min.)
ARTICHOKES			
Fresh, about 6 to 8 oz. ea.	1	9 to 11	5
(3-in. diameter)	2 plus ½ cup water	12½ to 15	5
Frozen, hearts	1 package (9 oz.)	7½ to 9	5
ASPARAGUS			
Fresh, cut into 1½-in. pieces	1 pounded plus ¼ cup water	7½ to 9½	5
Frozen, spears	1 package (10 oz.)	8 to 10½	5
BEANS, Green or Wax			
Fresh, cut into 1½-in. pieces	1 pound plus ¼ cup water	9½ to 12	5
Frozen	1 package (9 oz.)	9 to 12	5
BEETS			
Fresh, sliced	1½ to 2 pounds plus ¼ cup water	15½ to 18	5
BROCCOLI			
Fresh, cut into spears	1 pound plus ¼ cup water	9 to 11	5
Frozen, chopped or spears	1 package (10 oz.)	9½ to 12	5
BRUSSELS SPROUTS			
Fresh	1 pound plus ¼ cup water	8 to 10½	5
Frozen	1 package (10 oz.)	11 to 13½	5

VEGETABLE	AMT.	COOK TIME (in min.)	STANDING TIME (in min.)
CABBAGE, Fresh			
Chopped or Shredded	4 cups (about 1 lb.) plus 1/4 cup water	9 1/2 to 12	5
Wedges	4 (about 1 lb.) plus 1/4 cup water	9 to 11	5
CARROTS, sliced 1/2-in thick			
Fresh	1 pound plus 1/4 cup water	10 1/2 to 12 1/2	5
Frozen	1 package (10 oz.)	8 to 10 1/2	5
CAULIFLOWER			
Fresh, cut into flowerets	1 pound plus 1/4 cup water	9 1/2 to 12	5
whole	1 to 1 1/4 lb. plus 1/4 cup water	17 to 19 1/2	5
Frozen, flowerets	1 package (10 oz.)	8 to 10 1/2	5
CORN, Whole Kernel			
Frozen	1 package (10 oz.)	6 to 8	5
CORN, on the cob			
Fresh (remove husk and silk)	1 ear ⎯⎤ plus 2 to 4	3 to 4 1/2	5
	2 ears ⎥ tablespoons	4 1/2 to 6	5
	4 ears ⎯⎦ water	12 1/2 to 15	5
Frozen (rinse off any frost)	1 ear	5 to 6 1/2	5
	2 ears	7 1/2 to 9 1/2	5
	4 ears	14 to 16 1/2	5
EGGPLANT, Fresh			
Cubed	1 pound plus 1/4 cup water	10 1/2 to 12 1/2	5
Whole (pierce skin)	1 to 1 1/4 pounds	6 1/2 to 9	5
LIMA BEANS			
Frozen	1 package (10 oz.) plus 1/4 cup water	8 to 10 1/2	5
OKRA, Frozen			
Sliced	1 package (10 oz.)	7 1/2 to 9 1/2	5
Whole	1 package (10 oz.)	8 to 10 1/2	5
ONIONS			
Fresh, (small, whole)	8 to 10 plus 1/4 cup water (about 1 lb.)	9 1/2 to 12	5
PEAS, GREEN			
Fresh	1 1/2 pounds plus 1/4 cup water	7 1/2 to 9 1/2	5
Frozen	1 package (10 oz.)	8 to 10 1/2	5
PEAS, Snow (Peapods)			
Frozen	1 package (6 oz.)	6 1/2 to 8	5
PEAS and CARROTS			
Frozen	1 package (10 oz.)	8 to 10 1/2	5

VEGETABLE	AMT.	COOK TIME (in min.)	STANDING TIME (in min.)
SPINACH			
Fresh, leaf	1 pound plus ¼ cup water	8 to 10½	5
Frozen, leaf of chopped	1 package (10 oz.)	9½ to 12	5
SQUASH (Summer), sliced ½-in. thick			
Fresh	1 pound plus ¼ cup water	9½ to 12	5
Frozen	1 package (10 oz.)	7½ to 9½	5
SQUASH (Winter)			
Fresh, whole	1 (1 lb.)	9 to 11	7
(pierce skin)	2 (¾ lb. ea.)	11 to 13 ½	7
Frozen, whipped	1 package (12 oz.)	8 to 10	5
SUCCOTASH			
Frozen	1 package (10 oz.)	8 to 10½	5
VEGETABLES, mixed			
Frozen	1 package (10 oz.)	9½ to 12	5
ZUCCHINI, sliced ½-in. thick			
Fresh	1 pound plus ¼ cup water	9½ to 12	5
Frozen	1 package (10 oz.)	7½ to 9½	5

CANNED VEGETABLES MICROWAVING GUIDE

VEGETABLE	AMT.	COOK TIME (in min.)	
		UNDRAINED	DRAINED
VEGETABLES	8 oz.	2½ to 3	2 to 2½
ALL KINDS	15 oz.	3½ to 5	3 to 3½
	17 oz.	5 to 6	3½ to 4

PREPARING BAKED POTATOES

- Select potatoes of equal size and shape.
- Rinse potatoes; pat dry.
- Prick skins several times with fork to allow steam to escape and prevent bursting.
- Arrange in circular pattern on paper towel lined glass oven tray, equal distance apart.
- Heat according to chart.
- Let stand, covered, 5 minutes before serving.

POTATOES	AMT.	COOK TIME* (in min.)
Medium Baking	1	6 to 8
Potatoes	2	9 to 11
(about 6 oz. ea.)	4	12 to 15

Cook time will vary slightly with larger or smaller potatoes.

BLANCHING FRESH VEGETABLES GUIDE

VEGETABLE	AMT.	WATER	COOK TIME (in min.)
ASPARAGUS Cut, 2 inch pieces	1 lb.	¼ cup	3 to 4½
BEANS, GREEN Cut, 2 inch pieces	1 lb.	¼ cup	7½ to 9
BROCCOLI Cut, spears	1 to 1¼ lbs.	¼ cup	6 to 7½
CARROTS Sliced	1 lb.	¼ cup	6 to 7½
CAULIFLOWER Cut, flowerets	1½ to 1¾ lbs.	¼ cup	4½ to 6
SPINACH, leaves	1 to 1¾ lbs.	—	3 to 4½
ZUCCHINI Cut, ½ inch pieces	1 lb.	¼ cup	4½ to 6

HOW TO BLANCH FRESH VEGETABLES

- Prepare vegetables ; wash and slice or chop as directed.
- Measure amount to be blanched into medium casserole.
- Add water if directed; cover and heat for time indicated in chart, until vegetables are an even bright color throughout.
- Stir once.
- Plunge vegetables immediately into ice water.
- Pat dry with paper towel to absorb excess moisture.
- Package in freezer container or poly bags.
- Label, date and freeze immediately.

PREPARING DRIED BEANS AND PEAS

- Bring beans and hot water to a boil.
- Heat for time indicated in chart, until tender.
- Let stand, covered, 10 minutes.

DRIED VEGETABLES	CONTAINER	AMT. of HOT WATER	COOK TIME (in min.)
Black-eyed peas (1 lb.)	3-qt. casserole dish	2½ quarts	30 to 35
Kidney beans, Lima beans (small, 1 lb.)	3-qt. casserole dish	2 quarts	40 to 45
Northern beans (1 lb.)	3-qt. casserole dish	2 quarts	80 to 85
Lima beans (large, 1 lb.)	3-qt. casserole dish	2½ quarts	40 to 45
Split peas. (1 lb.)	3-qt. casserole dish	1½ quarts	40 to 45
Lentils (1 lb.)	3-qt. casserole dish	1½ quarts	40 to 45

ARTICHOKES FOR TWO

Approx. Cooking Time: 20 min.
Yield: 2 servings

- **¹/₃ cup butter or margarine**
  Garlic salt
- **2 fresh artichokes (8 oz. ea.)**
- **1 lemon, thinly sliced and halved**
- **¹/₄ teaspoon paprika**
- **¹/₄ teaspoon parsely flakes**

1. In small bowl, heat butter 2 to 3 minutes until melted; reserve 1 tablespoon. Into remaining butter, add garlic salt.
2. Cut stem off artichoke; trim tips of leaves, then rinse.
3. Place lemon in between leaves; arrange artichokes in individual custard cups and pour butter mixture over each. Cover with plastic wrap and heat 14 to 17 minutes. Combine reserved melted butter with remaining ingredients.
4. Sprinkle over cooked artichokes; let stand, covered, 5 minutes before serving.

CORN RELISH

Approx. Cooking Time: 10 min.
Yield: 6 servings

- **Water**
- **2 cans (12 oz. ea.) whole kernel corn, drained (reserve liquid)**
- **¹/₂ cup chopped celery**
- **¹/₂ cup diced green pepper**
- **¹/₄ cup finely chopped onion**
- **2 to 3 tablespoons sugar**
- **1 tablespoon cornstarch**
- **¹/₃ cup cider vinegar**
- **2 tablespoons diced pimento**

1. In 4-cup glass measure, add enough water to reserved liquid to equal 1¹/₄ cups. Add celery, green pepper, onion and sugar, heat 4 to 6 minutes.
2. Stir in cornstarch blended with vinegar and heat 4 to 5 minutes until mixture is slightly thickened, stirring occasionally.
3. Add corn and pimento; chill before serving.

CARAWAY CABBAGE

Approx. Cooking Time: 16 min.
Yield: 6 servings

- **¼ cup butter or margarine**
- **1 small head cabbage, cut into 6 wedges (about 1½ lbs.)**
- **¼ teaspoon caraway seeds**
- **¼ cup water**

1. In 10 x 6 x 2-inch baking dish, heat butter 1 to 2 minutes until melted.
2. Brush cabbage with butter and arrange wide edge towards rim, in same dish; sprinkle with caraway seeds and water.
3. Heat, covered, 12 to 14 minutes until cabbage is almost tender; let stand, covered, 5 minutes before serving.

CHEESY VEGETABLE CASSEROLE

Approx. Cooking Time: 28 min.
Yield: 6 servings

- **4 medium onions, sliced (about 1 lb.)**
- **1 teaspoon salt**
- **½ teaspoon basil**
- **¼ teaspoon pepper**
- **3 tablespoons butter or margarine**
- **½ cup seasoned dry bread crumbs Paprika**
- **4 medium tomatoes (about 1½ lbs.), sliced**
- **6 slices American cheese (1 oz. ea.)**

1. In medium glass bowl, heat, covered, onions 6 to 8 minutes, stirring once; stir in salt, basil and pepper.
2. In small glass bowl, heat butter 1 to 2 minutes until melted; stir in bread crumbs and paprika. In 2-quart casserole dish, alternately layer half the tomatoes, onions and cheese; top with remaining tomatoes and onions. Cover and heat for 15 to 18 minutes giving dish ¼ turn every 5 minutes.
3. Top with remaining cheese, then bread crumb mixture; let stand, covered, 5 minutes before serving.

BROCCOLI EGG DIVINE

Approx. Cooking Time: 13 min.
Yield: 6 servings

- **1 package (1¼ oz.) hollandaise sauce mix**
- **1 pound fresh broccoli spears, cooked***
- **4 hard-cooked eggs, chopped**
- **2 slices Swiss cheese, cubed**
- **¼ cup dry bread crumbs**
- **2 tablespoons butter or margarine, melted Paprika**

1. In 2-cup glass measure, mix hollandaise sauce mix according to package directions. Heat 3 to 5 minutes until sauce is thickened, stirring once.
2. In glass pie plate, arrange broccoli in spoke fashion, stems towards outside of dish; top with eggs and cheese. Pour sauce over cheese and top with bread crumbs blended with butter and paprika.
3. Heat, covered, 7 to 9 minutes until heated through. Let stand, covered, 5 minutes before seving.

*Substitution: *Use 2 packages (10 oz. ea.) frozen broccoli spears, cooked for fresh broccoli.*

MUSHROOM SAUTÉ

Approx. Cooking Time: 7 min.
Yield: 3 to 4 servings

- **½ pound fresh mushrooms, cleaned and sliced**
- **⅓ cup butter**
- **1 clove garlic, peeled and minced Parmesan cheese**

1. Combine all ingredients, except Parmesan cheese, in an 8-inch round baking dish. Cover with wax paper and heat for 6 to 7 minutes. Stir once.
2. Serve as side dish, sprinkling the top with Parmesan cheese, if desired.

GREEN BEANS SUPREME

Approx. Cooking Time: 9 min.
Yield: 3 to 4 servings

> **2 tablespoons melted butter or margarine, divided**
> **¼ cup dry bread crumbs**
> **2 tablespoons grated Cheddar cheese**
> **1 tablespoon all-purpose flour**
> **1½ teaspoons minced onion**
> **Salt and pepper to taste**
> **¼ teaspoon grated lemon peel**
> **2 tablespoons water**
> **½ cup sour cream**
> **1 can (16 oz.) green beans, drained**

1. Stir in 1 tablespoon of melted butter with bread crumbs and cheese. Set aside.
2. Combine flour, onion, salt, pepper and lemon peel with 1 tablespoon melted butter in 2-cup glass measure and heat for 1 to 1½ minutes.
3. Stir in 2 tablespoons water and sour cream. Mix with green beans and spoon mixture into a small casserole dish. Heat, uncovered, for 3 to 5 minutes.
4. Sprinkle with buttered bread crumbs and cheese mixture. Heat for 1 to 2 minutes.

RATATOUILLE

Approx. Cooking Time: 37 min.
Yield: 8 servings

> **2 medium onions, sliced**
> **1 medium green pepper, sliced**
> **⅓ cup oil**
> **2 cloves garlic, finely chopped**
> **1 medium eggplant (about 1½ lbs.), peeled and cut into ½-inch pieces**
> **3 medium tomatoes (about 1 lb.), chopped**
> **2 medium zucchini (about 1 lb.), thinly sliced**
> **1 cup vegetable juice cocktail or tomato juice**
> **2 teaspoons each basil and parsely flakes**
> **1 teaspoon salt**
> **¼ teaspoon pepper**

1. In 3-quart casserole dish, combine onions, green pepper, oil and garlic; heat , covered 6 to 8 minutes, stirring once.
2. Add remaining ingredients and heat, covered, 27 to 30 minutes until vegetables are tender, stirring occasionally. Let stand, covered, 5 minutes before serving.

ORANGE GLAZED CARROTS

Approx. Cooking Time: 12 min.
Yield: 4 servings

> **1 pound carrots, sliced ½-inch thick**
> **¼ cup orange juice**
> **3 tablespoons honey**
> **3 tablespoons butter or margarine**
> **½ teaspoon grated lemon peel (optional)**
> **¼ teaspoon salt**
> **Dash ground nutmeg**

1. In 2-quart casserole dish, combine carrots and orange juice; heat, covered, 10 to 12 minutes until carrots are tender, stirring once.
2. Stir in remaining ingredients: let stand, covered, 4 to 5 minutes before serving.

OKRA CREOLE

Approx. Cooking Time: 30 min.
Yield: 6 servings

> **1 medium onion, sliced**
> **¼ cup butter or margarine**
> **2 packages (10 oz. ea.) frozen sliced okra**
> **1 can (16 oz.) stewed tomatoes, chopped**
> **½ teaspoon Worcestershire sauce**
> **¼ teaspoon hot pepper sauce**
> **Salt and pepper to taste**

1. In 2-quart casserole dish, heat onion and butter 3 to 5 minutes until onion is tender.
2. Add okra, tomatoes, Worcestershire and pepper sauce; heat, covered 22 to 25 minutes until vegetables are tender, stirring twice. Season with salt and pepper; let stand, covered, 5 minutes before serving.

HERB BAKED TOMATOES

Approx. Cooking Time: 3 min.
Yield: 4 servings

 **3 tablespoons seasoned dry
   bread crumbs
 2 tablespoons butter or margarine, melted
 2 tablespoons grated Parmesan
   cheese
 1/2 teaspoon oregano or basil
 2 medium tomatoes, cut in half**

1. Combine bread crumbs, butter, cheese
   and oregano.
2. In 8-inch square baking dish, arrange
   tomato halves; top with bread crumb
   mixture. Heat, covered, 2 to 3 minutes
   until tomatoes are tender, turning once.
   Let stand 5 minutes before serving.

GREEN BEANS AMANDINE

Approx. Cooking Time: 21 min.
Yield: 4 servings

 **1/4 cup slivered almonds
 3 tablespoons butter or margarine
 1 1/4 to 1 1/2 pounds fresh green beans,
   cut into 1 1/2-inch pieces
 1/4 cup water
 1/2 teaspoon salt
   Dash ground nutmeg (optional)**

1. In glass measure, heat almonds and
   butter 4 to 6 minutes until almonds are
   lightly browned; reserve
2. In 2-quart casserole dish, combine beans
   and water; heat, covered, 12 to 15 minutes until beans are tender, stirring once.
3. Add remaining ingredients, almonds
   and butter; let stand, covered, 5 minutes
   before serving

HONEY ACORN SQUASH

Approx. Cooking Time: 16 min.
Yield: 4 servings

 **1 acorn squash (about 3/4 lb. ea.)
 2 tablespoons honey
 2 teaspoons butter or margarine
 1/8 teaspoon grated lemon peel**

1. Pierce skin of squash several times,
   arrange on paper towel lined glass oven
   tray. Heat 6 to 8 minutes, turning squash
   over once; let stand 5 minutes. Cut
   squash in half; scoop out seeds. In 10 x
   6 x 2-inch baking dish, arrange squash,
   cut-side up.
2. Top with honey, butter and lemon. Heat,
   covered, 6 to 8 minutes until squash is
   tender; let stand, covered, 5 minutes
   before serving.

For FRUIT'N HONEY SQUASH, *use 2
tablespoons finely chopped apple, 1 tablespoon flaked coconut, 2 tablespoons honey
and 7 tablespoons butter.*

WILTED SPINACH SALAD

Approx. Cooking Time: 6 min.
Yield: 2 servings

 **1/2 pound fresh spinach
 3 slices bacon, cooked and crumbled (reserve drippings)
 1 1/2 tablespoons pimento, finely
   chopped
 3 tablespoons water
 3 tablespoons wine vinegar
 1 1/2 tablespoons onion, finely
   chopped
 1 tablespoon sugar
   Dash of pepper to taste**

1. Wash spinach carefully, removing bruised
   pieces and all thick stems. Set aside.
2. Combine onions and bacon fat in small
   glass measure and heat for 1 to 2 minutes
   until onions are slightly browned.
3. Add remaining ingredients to onion
   mixture and heat for 2 to 4 minutes until
   liquid comes to a boil.
4. Just before serving, pour hot dressing
   over spinach leaves, sprinkle with
   crumbled bacon, toss lightly and serve
   immediately.

BUTTERED CRUMB POTATOES

Approx. Coking Time: 12 min.
Yield: 4 servings

- **4 medium potatoes, peeled (about 4 oz. ea.)**
- **2 tablespoons butter or margarine, melted**
- **1/2 cup seasoned dry bread crumbs**

1. Roll potatoes in butter, then in bread crumbs.
2. Arrange potatoes in baking dish; drizzle with remaining butter. Heat 10 to 12 minutes until potatoes are tender; let stand, covered, 4 minutes before serving.

STUFFED ONIONS FLORENTINE

Approx. Cooking Time: 37 min.
Yield: 6 servings

- **6 large Spanish onions (about 3 1/2 lbs.)**
- **1/3 cup water**
- **1/2 pound pork sausage, cooked and crumbled**
- **1 package (10 oz.) frozen chopped spinach, thawed and drained**
- **1 egg**
- **3/4 cup shredded Cheddar or Swiss cheese**
- **6 tablespoons buttered bread crumbs**

1. Peel onions; cut 1/2-inch slice off sprout end and just enough off the root end to sit flat. In shallow baking dish, arrange onions, add water and heat 17 to 20 minutes until onions are partially cooked. Carefully remove centers of onion, leaving a 1/4 to 1/2-inch shell; chop 1/4 cup onion centers.
2. In glass bowl, combine 1/4 cup chopped onion, crumbled sausage, spinach and egg. Heat 6 to 8 minutes, stirring twice; drain.
3. Stir in cheese. Stuff onions with spinach mixture and arrange in baking dish; top with bread crumbs. Heat, covered, 9 to 10 minutes until heated enough. Let stand, covered, 7 minutes before serving.

ZUCCHINI PARMESAN

Approx. Cooking Time: 13 min.
Yield: 4 servings

- **4 medium zucchini, sliced into 1-in. pieces (about 1 1/2 lbs.)**
- **1/4 cup grated Parmesan cheese**
- **1 can (8 oz.) tomato sauce**
- **1/2 cup shredded Mozzarella cheese**

1. In 8-inch round baking dish, combine zucchini, Parmesan cheese and tomato sauce; heat, covered, 12 to 13 minutes until zucchini is tender, stirring once.
2. Sprinkle with mozzarella cheese and let stand, covered, 5 minutes before serving.

GARDEN SUCCOTASH

Approx. Cooking Time: 19 min.
Yield: 6 servings

- **1 package (10 oz.) frozen lima beans**
- **1 package (10 oz.) frozen whole kernel corn**
- **2 tablespoons chopped pimento (optional)**
- **1/4 cup milk**
- **3 tablespoons butter or margarine**
- **1 teaspoon salt**
  Dash pepper

1. In 2-quart casserole dish, combine lima beans, corn and pimento; heat, covered, 14 to 17 minutes until vegetables are tender, stirring once.
2. Stir in remaining ingredients; heat, covered, 1 to 2 minutes until heated through.

HOT GERMAN POTATO SALAD

Approx. Cooking Time: 16 min.
Yield: 4 servings

- **4 slices bacon, diced**
- **1/4 cup finely chopped onion**
- **2 teaspoons flour**
- **1/3 cup cider vinegar**
- **2 tablespoons brown sugar**
- **1/4 teaspoon celery seed**
  Salt and pepper to taste
- **4 medium potatoes, baked, peeled and sliced***

1. In 10 x 6 x 2-inch baking dish, heat bacon and onion 5 to 7 1/2 minutes, stirring occasionally.
2. Stir in flour, vinegar, sugar, celery seed, salt and pepper; heat 1 to 2 minutes until slightly thickened, stirring once.
3. Add potatoes and heat 4 to 6 minutes until heated through, stirring once. Serve warm.

*Substitution: *Use 2 cans (16. oz. ea.) sliced potatoes, drained for baked potatoes.*

CANDIED SWEET POTATOES

Approx. Cooking Time: 16 min.
Yield: 6 servings

- **1/4 cup butter or margarine**
- **2 cans (16 oz. ea.) sweet potatoes or yams, drained**
- **1 egg**
- **1/2 cup milk**
- **2 tablespoons brown sugar**
- **2 tablespoons molasses**
- **1/2 teaspoon ground cinnamon**
- **1/4 teaspoon ground nutmeg**
  Dash ground cloves
- **1/2 cup miniature marshmallows (optional)**

1. In 1 1/2-quart casserole dish, heat butter 1 to 2 minutes until melted. Add sweet potatoes, egg, milk, sugar, molasses, cinnamon, nutmeg and cloves; mash until smooth.
2. Cover with plastic wrap and heat for 12 to 14 minutes until heated through.
3. Top with marshmallows. Heat, uncovered, 1 minute.

BAKED STUFFED POTATOES

Approx. Cooking Time: 8 min.
Yield: 4 servings

- **4 medium potatoes, baked**
- **1/2 cup shredded Cheddar cheese**
- **1/3 to 1/2 cup milk**
- **2 tablespoons butter or margarine**
- **1 egg**
  Salt and pepper to taste
  Paprika

1. Cut a thin slice (lengthwise) from top of each potato. Scoop out potato, leaving a thin shell. Combine potato, cheese, milk, butter, egg, salt and pepper; mash until smooth.
2. Spoon potato mixture into shell; sprinkle with paprika. Heat on paper towel lined glass oven tray 6 to 8 minutes until heated through.

Note: For TWO servings, *follow above procedure; halve all ingredients (use whole egg). Heat 3 to 5 minutes.*

POTATO DUMPLINGS

Approx. Cooking Time: 14 min.
Yield: 4 to 6 servings

- **2 quarts hot water or broth**
- **2 cups hot mashed potatoes**
- **1/2 cup flour**
- **1 egg**
- **1/2 teaspoon salt**
- **1/4 teaspoon parsley flakes**
- **1/8 teaspoon pepper**
  Dash ground nutmeg

1. In 3-quart casserole, heat water, covered, 10 minutes until water is boiling.
2. Meanwhile, combine remaining ingredients; drop by heaping tablespoons into water. Heat 3 to 4 minutes until dumplings float; drain.

SWISS SCALLOPED CORN

Approx. Cooking Time: 20 to 25 min.
Yield: 6 servings

- 3 **slices bacon, cooked and crumbled**
- 2 **cans (16 oz.) whole kernel corn, drained**
- 1 **cup shredded Swiss cheese (about 1/4 lb.)**
- 1/2 **teaspoon onion powder**
- 1/8 **teaspoon pepper**
- 1 **tablespoon flour**
- 1 **egg**
- 1 **can (5 1/2 oz.) evaporated milk**
- 1/4 **cup dry bread crumbs**
- 1 **tablespoon butter or margarine, melted**
  Dash of paprika

1. In 1 1/2-quart casserole combine bacon, corn, cheese, onion, pepper, flour, egg and milk. Top with bread crumbs blended with butter and paprika.
2. Heat 20 to 25 minutes until corn is set, giving dish 1/4 turn every 5 minutes. Let stand, covered, 5 minutes before serving.

FANCY GREEN BEANS

Approx. Cooking Time: 25 min.
Yields: 6 servings

- 2 **packages (9 oz.) frozen French-style green beans**
- 1 **can (10 3/4 oz.) condensed cream of mushroom soup**
- 1 **can (3 oz.) French fried onions**

1. In 2-quart casserole dish, heat beans, covered, 14 to 16 minutes until beans are tender, stirring twice.
2. Stir in soup and 1/2 onion pieces; top with remaining onion pieces. Heat for 7 to 9 minutes.
3. Let stand 5 minutes before serving.

BAKED BEANS

Approx. Cooking Time: 20 to 24 min.
Yield: 6 servings

- 3 **slices bacon, diced**
- 1/2 **cup chopped green pepper or onion**
- 2 **cans (16 oz. ea.) pork and beans**
- 1/4 **cup molasses**
- 1/4 **cup catsup**
- 1 **tablespoon prepared mustard**
- 1/2 **teaspoon Worcestershire sauce**
  Dash hot pepper sauce

1. In 1 1/2-quart casserole dish, heat bacon and green pepper 4 1/2 to 6 minutes until bacon is crisp. Drain.
2. Stir in remaining ingredients and cover.
3. Heat 16 to 18 minutes until mixture is bubbly, giving dish 1/4 turn every 5 minutes.

Pictured on the following page: Barbecued Beef Sandwiches (Hamburger Rolls & Bread), Tip-Top ▶ Hamburgers, Open Faced Sandwiches with Gravy,

Sandwiches

OPEN FACED TUNA

Approx. Cooking Time: 5 min.
Yield: 4 servings

- **1 can (7 oz.) tuna, drained and flaked**
- **1/3 cup mayonnaise**
  Celery seed
  Onion powder
  Salt and pepper
- **4 slices whole wheat bread, toasted**
- **4 thin slices tomato**
- **4 slices American cheese**

1. Combine tuna, mayonnaise, celery seed, onion powder, salt and pepper. Spread on toast; top with tomato.
2. On paper plate, heat sandwiches 2 to 3 minutes; top with cheese. Heat 1 to 2 minutes until cheese is melted.

MINI-PIZZA SNACKS

Approx. Cooking Time: 2 min.
Yield: 2 servings

- **2 English muffins, split and toasted**
- **1/4 to 1/2 cup spaghetti sauce**
- **1/4 cup shredded Mozzarella cheese**
  Oregano

1. On paper plate, arrange muffins; spread with spaghetti sauce. Top with cheese and season with oregano.
2. Heat 1 to 2 minutes until cheese is melted, turning dish a 1/2 turn after 1 minute.

Note: For ONE serving, *follow above procedure; halve all ingredients. Heat 1/2 to 1 minute.*

CHEESY MEAT LOAF SANDWICH

Approx. Cooking Time: 4 min.
Yield: 4 servings

- **Chili sauce**
- **8 slices rye bread**
- **8 thin slices cooked meat loaf**
- **4 slices Muenster cheese, halved**

1. Spread chili sauce on bread. On four slices, place meat loaf and cheese; top with remaining bread.
2. Wrap each sandwich in paper napkin; arrange on glass oven tray. Heat 2 to 4 minutes until heated through.

TIP-TOP HAMBURGERS

Approx. Cooking Time: 7 min.
Yield: 4 servings

- **1 pound ground beef**
- **4 slices each cheese, onion and tomato**
- **4 hamburger rolls**
  Catsup or creamy Russian dressing

1. Shape ground beef into 4 patties (about 4-inches in diameter). In 8-inch square baking dish, arrange patties and heat 5 to 7 minutes turning patties over and draining liquid once.
2. Top with cheese; let stand, covered, 5 minutes. Place each hamburger in roll and top, with remaining ingredients, as desired.

Note: For TWO servings, *follow above procedure. Halve all ingredients; heat patties 2 to 3 minutes.*

BARBECUED BEEF SANDWICHES

Approx. Cooking Time: 4 min.
Yield: 4 servings

- **1/2 to 3/4 pound sliced cooked roast beef**
- **8 slices rye bread or 4 hamburger rolls**
- **1/4 to 1/2 cup barbecue or chili sauce**

1. Arrange 1/2 beef on 4 slices bread; spread generously with barbecue sauce. Top with remaining beef, then bread.
2. Wrap each sandwich in paper napkin; arrange on glass oven tray. Heat 3 to 4 minutes until heated through.

Note: For TWO sandwiches, *follow above procedure. Halve all ingredients; heat 1 1/2 to 2 minutes.*

RYE DOGS

Approx. Cooking Time: 9 min.
Yield: 2 servings

> 1   **can (8 oz.) pork and beans**
> 1   **tablespoon sweet pickle
>   relish or catsup**
> 4   **frankfurters
>   Mustard**
> 2   **slices rye bread**
> 2   **slices bacon, cooked
>   and crumbled**
> 1/4 **cup shredded Cheddar cheese**

1. In small glass bowl, heat beans and relish, covered, 2 to 3 minutes until heated through, stirring once.
2. Along one side of each frankfurter, make deep slits every 3/4-inch. On paper towel lined paper plate, arrange franks cut-side out. Heat 3 1/2 to 4 minutes until heated through and curled.
   Spread mustard on bread; place on serving plate.
3. Arrange two franks on each slice of bread to form ring. Fill ring with beans; top with bacon and cheese. Heat 1 to 2 minutes until cheese begins to melt.

Variation: *Arrange cooked frankfurter on toasted English muffin half; fill center with heated sauerkraut and top with poppy seeds.*

TEXAS TASTERS

Approx. Cooking Time: 10 min.
Yield: 2 servings

> 8   **slices bacon**
> 4   **frankfurters**
> 1   **slice American cheese, cut into
>   thin strips**
> 4   **frankfurter rolls**

1. In 10 x 6 x 2-inch baking dish, heat bacon between 2 layers of paper towels, 3 to 4 minutes until partially cooked.
   Make lengthwise slit in each frankfurter, leaving 1/2-inch uncut on each end; make an "X" cut in each end.
2. Stuff slit with cheese; wrap 2 slices of bacon around each frankfurter and secure with wooden toothpicks.

3. Discard paper towels from baking dish and arrange frankfurters in dish. Heat 3 to 5 minutes until heated through. Remove toothpicks and serve in split-rolls.

INTERNATIONAL SANDWICH

Approx. Cooking Time: 3 to 4 min.
Yield: 1 sandwich

> 1   **thick (1 in.) slice French bread
>   Butter**
> 1   **slice bologna**
> 1   **slice salami**
> 1/2 **cup sauerkraut***
> 1/2 **cup grated Mozzarella cheese**

1. Spread bread with butter. Cut bologna and salami in halves. Alternate the half-slices over bread, then top with sauerkraut. Sprinkle cheese over top.
2. Place sandwich on paper or china plate. Heat for 3 to 4 minutes, giving plate 1/4 turn after 2 minutes.

* *8 oz. can sauerkraut, drained, makes 2 sandwiches.*

SUPER-SURPRISE BURGERS

Approx. Cooking Time: 10 min.
Yield: 4 servings

> 1   **pound ground beef**
> 1/2 **teaspoon salt**
> 1/2 **teaspoon pepper
>   Surprise Fillings***
> 4   **hamburger rolls**

1. Combine ground beef, salt and pepper; shape into 8 thin patties. Arrange Surprise Filling on 4 patties; top with remaining patties, sealing edges tightly.
2. In 8-inch square baking dish, arrange burgers; heat, covered with wax paper 7 to 10 minutes, giving dish 1/4 turn after 4 minutes. Let stand, covered, 5 minutes before serving in split rolls.

*Surprise Fillings:
Use one of the following: cheese, onion or tomato slices, sliced mushrooms, pickle slices or chopped olives.

Memo

Pictured on the following page: Banana Nut Coffee Cake. and Cherry Brunch Rolls ▶

Breads, Muffins and Coffee Cakes

SPECIAL HINTS FOR BAKING QUICK BREADS, MUFFINS AND COFFEE CAKES

- Prepare batter according to package or recipe directions.
- Use microwave-safe containers as indicated in charts or recipes.
- Grease bottom of baking dish when cake will be served from dish.
- Grease and line bottom of baking dishes with wax paper if inverting to remove from dish. DO NOT GREASE AND FLOUR DISHES.

- Check quick breads and coffee cakes several times through cooking. If some areas are cooking faster than others, turn dish ¼ turn; continue cooking.
- Test for doneness with a toothpick inserted near the center—it should come out clean.
- Let stand on flat surface, covered, 10 to 15 minutes to finish baking.
- Turn out of dish and carefully peel off wax paper.
- To enhance the appearance of quick breads, top with one of the following: Toasted coconut, cinnamon and sugar, or chopped nuts.

PREPARING BREAD MIXES

ITEM	CONTAINER	COOK TIME (in min.)	STANDING TIME, COVERED (in min.)
Coffee cake (14 oz.)	8-in. round dish	9 to 11	10
Fruit Variety (16 to 19 oz.)	8-in. round dish	11 to 13	10
Cornbread (12 oz.)	8-in. round dish	7 to 9	10
Gingerbread	8-in. round or square dish	7 to 9	5
Quick Bread (14½ to 17 oz.)	glass loaf dish, bottom lined with wax paper	10 to 12	15

CHILI CHEESE CORN BREAD

Approx. Cooking Time: 8 min.
Yield: 4 to 5 servings

1 egg
³/₄ teaspoon salt
¹/₂ cup sour cream
2 tablespoons melted butter or margarine
¹/₂ cup yellow corn meal
¹/₂ cup whole kernel corn, drained
¹/₂ tablespoon baking powder
Dash of Tabasco sauce
Dash of pepper
1 to 2 oz. canned green chilies, drained and chopped
³/₄ cup shredded sharp Cheddar cheese

1. Blend all ingredients, except green chilies and cheese, in a large glass bowl.
2. Grease a small oblong baking dish with butter and pour half of the batter into the dish.
3. Sprinkle batter with green chilies and ¹/₄ cup of cheese. Reserve remaining cheese. Pour remaining batter over the chilies and cheese.
4. Top with remaining cheese and heat, uncovered, for 7 to 8 minutes. Let stand 3 to 5 minutes before serving.

CORN BREAD

Approx. Cooking Time: 6 min.
Yield: 3 to 4 servings

¹/₂ cup sifted flour
¹/₂ cup yellow corn meal
1 tablespoon sugar
¹/₂ teaspoon baking powder
¹/₂ teaspoon baking soda
¹/₂ teaspoon salt
1 egg
¹/₂ cup sour milk
2 tablespoons oil

1. Sift flour, corn meal, sugar, baking powder, baking soda and salt together into a medium mixing bowl.
2. Beat egg in a medium mixing bowl and add sour milk and oil. Blend well. Combine milk egg mixture with flour mixture; stir well.

3. Pour batter into an 8-inch round dish. Heat, uncovered, for 4 to 6 minutes, giving dish ¹/₄ turn every 2 minutes.

SIMPLE COFFEE CAKE

Approx. Cooking Time: 8 to 9 min.
Yield: 1 cake

2 cups unsifted all purpose flour
¹/₂ cup sugar
3 teaspoons baking powder
¹/₂ teaspoon salt
2 eggs, beaten
¹/₂ cup cooking oil
¹/₂ cup milk

1. In mixing bowl, combine flour, baking powder and salt. Make a well in center of dry mixture.
2. Combine eggs, oil and milk. Add all at once to dry mixture and stir just to moisten.
3. Pour into greased 8-inch round dish and sprinkle with topping (below).
4. Heat for 8 to 9 minutes, giving dish ¹/₄ turn every 2 minutes.

Topping: *Blend 2 tablespoons flour, 1 tablespoon cinnamon, 1 tablespoon cocoa, ¹/₃ cup sugar and ¹/₄ cup cold butter until crumbly.*

MARMALADE GINGERBREAD

Approx. Cooking Time: 9 min.
Yield: 8 servings

1 package (14 oz.) gingerbread mix
³/₄ cup orange juice
¹/₂ cup orange marmalade

1. Combine gingerbread mix, orange juice and marmalade; blend according to package directions.
2. Pour into greased 8-inch round baking dish; heat 7¹/₂ to 8¹/₂ minutes giving dish ¹/₄ turn every 3 minutes. Let stand, covered, 10 minutes. Store, covered, until ready to serve.

CRISPY CROUTONS

Approx. Cooking Time: 10 min.
Yield: 3 cups

1/3 cup butter or margarine
6   slices pumpernickel or rye
bread

1. In small glass bowl, heat butter 1 1/2 minutes until melted. Brush butter onto bread (one side only); cut bread into small cubes.
2. In oblong baking dish, arrange bread; drizzle with remaining butter. Heat 7 1/2 to 9 minutes until bread is crispy, stirring twice. Let stand 10 minutes; store, covered, until ready to serve.

QUICK MUFFINS

Approx. Cooking Time: 4 min.
Yield: 6 muffins

6 tablespoons milk
1 egg
1 tablespoon cooking oil
1 cup buttermilk biscuit mix
2 tablespoons sugar

1. Combine milk, egg and oil in small bowl; blend well.
2. Sift together biscuit mix and sugar, add to milk-egg mixture. Stir just until flour is moistened.
3. Divide mixture into 6 custard cups or microwave safe muffin pan.
4. Heat 4 minutes, giving pan 1/4 turn or rearranging cups after 2 minutes.

CHERRY BRUNCH ROLLS

Approx. Cooking Time: 5 min.
Yield: 10 rolls

1/4 cup chopped maraschino cherries
1 cup brown sugar
1/4 cup flaked coconut
1/4 teaspoon ground cinnamon
1 can (10 oz.) refrigerated biscuits
1/3 cup butter or margarine, melted

1. Combine cherries, 1/2 cup brown sugar, coconut and cinnamon; sprinkle into 8-inch round baking dish with small glass inverted in center to form ring shape.
2. Dip each biscuit into melted butter and then in remaining brown sugar. Arrange biscuits on top of cherry mixture; sprinkle remaining sugar over ring. Heat 4 to 5 minutes.
3. Remove glass; let stand, covered, 5 minutes before inverting on serving platter. Store, covered, until ready to serve.

BOSTON BROWN BREAD

Approx. Cooking Time: 8 to 10 min.
Yield: 1 ring loaf

1 cup buttermilk
1/3 cup molasses
1/2 cup raisins
1/2 teaspoon baking powder
1/2 teaspoon baking soda
1/2 teaspoon salt
1/2 cup all-purpose flour
1/2 cup whole wheat flour
1/2 cup yellow cornmeal

1. Combine buttermilk and molasses; stir in raisins, baking powder, baking soda and salt. Add flours and cornmeal, stirring only until moistened. Pour batter into greased 9-inch straight-sided ring mold.
2. Cover with plastic wrap.
3. Heat 8 to 10 minutes. Let stand covered 10 minutes.
4. Remove from container. Store, covered, until ready to serve.

PECAN BUNS

Approx. Cooking Time: 8 to 9 min.
Yield: 8 buns

- **½ cup brown sugar**
- **⅓ cup finely chopped pecans**
- **1 teaspoon ground cinnamon**
- **1 can (8 oz.) refrigerated crescent dinner rolls**
- **¼ cup butter or margarine, melted**

1. In small bowl, combine sugar, pecans and cinnamon. Unroll 2 sections of dough but do not separate. On each long rectangle, spoon 1 teaspoon butter and 1 tablespoon pecan mixture; re-roll. Cut each into quarters, forming 8 buns. Dip each bun into remaining butter and then into pecan mixture.
2. In 8-inch round baking dish, arrange rolls in ring (do not place any in center); sprinkle remaining pecan mixture over ring.
3. Heat 8 to 9 minutes, let stand, covered, 5 minutes before inverting onto platter. Cover until ready to serve.

CRANBERRY COFFEE CAKE

Approx. Cooking Time: 11 min.
Yield: 8 servings

- **1 can (8 oz.) whole berry cranberry sauce**
- **6 tablespoons sugar**
- **¼ cup chopped nuts (optional)**
- **1 tablespoon butter or margarine, melted**
- **2 cups buttermilk biscuit mix**
- **1 cup orange juice or apple juice**
- **1 egg**

1. Combine cranberry sauce, 4 tablespoons sugar, nuts and butter; spread into 8-inch round baking dish, bottom lined with wax paper.
2. Combine biscuit mix, juice, egg and remaining sugar blending until smooth. Pour batter over cranberry mixture; heat 10 to 11 minutes. Let stand, covered, 10 minutes before inverting onto platter; carefully peel off wax paper.
3. Store, covered, until ready to serve. If desired, drizzle with Glaze* just before serving.

*Glaze: *Combine 1 cup confectioners sugar, 1 to 2 tablespoons water and ½ teaspoon vanilla extract.*

BANANA NUT COFFEE CAKE

Approx. Cooking Time: 10 min.
Yield: 8 servings

- **¼ cup shortening, melted**
- **¼ cup milk**
- **1 egg**
- **½ cup mashed ripe banana (about 1)**
- **½ cup brown sugar**
- **1 cup all-purpose flour**
- **½ cup chopped nuts**
- **¾ teaspoon baking powder**
- **½ teaspoon salt**
- **¼ teaspoon baking soda**
- **Nut Topping**

1. Combine shortening, milk, egg, banana and sugar; add flour, nuts, baking powder, salt and baking soda, stirring only until flour is moistened.
2. Pour into greased 8-inch round baking dish; sprinkle with Nut Topping. Heat 9 to 10 minutes; let stand, covered, 10 minutes. Store, covered, until ready to serve.

Nut Topping: *Combine ¼ cup brown sugar, ¼ cup chopped nuts, 2 tablespoons flour and ⅛ teaspoon ground cinnamon; blend in 1 tablespoon softened butter or margarine*

Memo

Pictured on the following page: Pineapple Upside-Down Cake, Double Butterscotch Brownies, ▶
Devil's Food Cake, Coconut Lemon Meringue Pie

Sweets and Treats

SPECIAL HINTS FOR SUCCESSFUL CAKES AND CUPCAKES

Layer cakes are baked in single layers, one at a time. The entire mix can be microwaved in a greased large glass bowl, with an inverted glass in the center to form a tube shape, or 16-cup Bundt dish.

When baking cupcakes, use custard cups lined with cupcake paper or set cupcake paper in microwave oven safe Cupcaker. Fill only 1/2 full. Arrange cups on glass oven tray in circular pattern if not using cupcaker.

- Prepare batter according to package or recipe directions.
- Use containers as indicated in charts or recipes.
- Use a large glass bowl with an inverted glass in the center or Bundt dish when baking all the batter at one time. Turn dish 1/4 turn every 3 minutes..

- Grease and line bottom of baking dishes with wax paper if the cake will be inverted. DO NOT GREASE AND FLOUR DISHES.
- Use 2 cups batter for each layer. Do not fill any container more than 1/2 full.
- Heat layers one at a time.
- Test cake doneness with toothpick inserted near the center; it should come out clean. There may be moist spots on the surface that evaporate as the cake cools.
- Let stand on flat surface, covered, 10 minutes.
- Turn out of dish and carefully peel off waxed paper or cool in dish.
- Store, covered, until ready to serve.
- Frost, if desired, when completely cooled.

PREPARING CAKE MIXES

ITEM	CONTAINER	COOK TIME (in min.)
Basic Cake (17 to 18½ oz.)	8 or 9-inch round or square cake dish	4 to 6
Brownies (15 oz.) (cake-like or fudge-like)	9-inch round or square cake dish	8 to 11
Bundt-type cake (17 to 18½ oz.)	16-cup Bundt dish or straight sided ring mold	12 to 14
Cake Mix with pudding mix included (18¾ to 20¼ oz.)	8 or 9-in. round cake dish (2 cups batter)	6 to 8
	16-cup Bundt dish or straight sided ring mold	13 to 15
Cupcakes	Cupcake paper in individual custard cups or Cupcaker	
	1	1 to 1½
	2	1 to 2
	4	2 to 3
	6	3 to 4
Mix-in-Dish Cake (15 oz.)	8 or 9-in. round or square cake dish	8 to 10

PREPARING PUDDING AND PIE FILLING MIXES

- Combine ingredients according to package directions.
- Use a glass container twice the volume of the mix.
- Heat for time given in chart, stirring twice during the cooking.
- Serve chilled.

PUDDING AND PIE FILLING MIX	COOK TIME (in min.)
Regular Pudding and Pie Filling	
2 servings (about 3 to 4 oz.)	7 to 9
6 servings (about 5 to 5½ oz.)	11 to 13
Rice Pudding (3¾ oz.)	7 to 9
Egg Custard (3 oz.)	7 to 9
Tapioca Pudding (3¼ oz.)	7 to 9

PREPARING PIE CRUSTS (8 or 9-inch single crust)

- Lightly grease glass pie plate before lining with pastry.
- Before cooking, prick bottom and sides of pastry with fork and brush with dark corn syrup or vanilla (for sweet fillings), and Worcestershire or soy sauce (for nonsweet).
- If desired, substitute ½ cup whole wheat flour for ½ cup all-purpose flour when preparing pastry from scratch.
- For frozen crust, put into a 8 or 9-inch glass pie plate; heat ½ minute, then prick crust and brush (as directed above).
- Recipe for graham cracker crust was prepared with ¼ cup butter (softened), 1¼ cup crumbs and ¼ cup sugar.
- Let stand to cool (chill crumb crusts).

PIE CRUSTS	COOK TIME (in min.)
From Scratch or Mix	5 to 7
Frozen	6 to 8
Graham Cracker or Cookie Crumb	2 to 3

CHOCOLATE POUND CAKE

Approx. Cooking Time: 15 min.
Yield: 12 servings

- **1 package (18½ oz.) chocolate cake mix**
- **1 package (4½ oz.) instant chocolate pudding mix**
- **4 eggs**
- **1 cup water**
- **¼ cup oil**

1. In large bowl, combine all ingredients; with electric mixer, beat at medium speed 4 minutes.
2. In greased 16-cup Bundt dish, pour batter; heat 13 to 15 minutes, giving dish ¼ turn every 3 minutes. Let stand, covered, 15 minutes before inverting onto serving platter.

BUTTER CAKE

Approx. Cooking Time: 9 min.
Yield: 1 layer

- **⅔ cup sugar**
- **¼ cup butter or margarine, softened**
- **1 egg**
- **⅔ cup milk**
- **1 teaspoon vanilla extract**
- **1 cup all-purpose flour**
- **1½ teaspoons baking powder**
- **¼ teaspoon salt**

1. Cream together sugar and butter; add egg, milk and vanilla. Add remaining ingredients, stirring until smooth.
2. Pour batter into greased 8 or 9-inch round baking dish. Heat 7 to 8½ minutes; let stand, covered, 10 minutes. Store, covered, until cool.

Hint: *If inverting cake and then frosting, line bottom of dish with wax paper. Turn out of dish and cool completely before frosting.*

APPLE SPICE TARTS

Approx. Cooking Time: 11 min. per batch
Yield: 12 tarts

- **1 can (21 oz.) apple pie filling**
- **1/4 cup raisins (optional)**
- **1 package (18 oz.) spice cake mix**
- **2 eggs**
- **1 1/3 cups water**
  Sweetened whipped cream or whipped topping

1. In each of 12 greased custard cups (10 oz. ea.), spoon 1 1/2 tablespoons pie filling and 1 teaspoon raisins.
2. Prepare cake mix according to package directions. Spoon 1/2 cup batter into each cup.
3. Arrange four cups on glass oven tray in circular pattern. Heat 9 1/2 to 1 1/2 minutes until tarts are done, rearranging dishes twice. Let stand, covered, 10 minutes.
4. Repeat procedure twice with remaining ingredients. To serve, loosen edge of each tart and invert onto serving plate; garnish with whipped cream.

CREAMY CHEESE CAKE

Approx. Cooking Time: 11 to 12 min.
Yield: 8 servings

- **1 package (8 oz.) cream cheese, softened**
- **1/2 cup sugar**
- **1 egg**
- **1 teaspoon vanilla extract**
- **1 cup sour cream**
  9-inch graham cracker crumb crust, baked

1. Combine cream cheese, sugar, egg and vanilla until smooth; stir in sour cream.
2. Pour mixture into prepared crust; heat 11 to 12 minutes until center is almost set.
3. Chill at least 3 hours or overnight.

Variation:
For CHOCOLATE Cheese cake, *add 1 packet (1 oz.) pre-melted unsweetened chocolate to cream cheese mixture; increase sugar to 2/3 cup.*

CRANBERRY-ORANGE SPICE CAKE

Approx. Cooking Time: 17 to 19 min.
Yield: 1 (10-in.) tube cake

- **1/2 cup butter, softened**
- **1 cup sugar**
- **1 egg**
- **1 1/2 cups unsifted all-purpose flour**
- **1/4 teaspoon salt**
- **1 teaspoon baking soda**
- **1 teaspoon ground cinnamon**
- **1/2 teaspoon ground cloves**
- **1 jar (14 oz.) cranberry orange relish**
- **1/2 cup raisins**
- **1/2 cup coarsely chopped walnuts**

1. In large mixing bowl place butter, sugar and egg. Beat well with medium speed of mixer until fluffy.
2. Add flour, salt, baking soda, cinnamon and cloves. Blend, using low speed, until moistened. Add relish, raisins and nuts. Mix until blended.
3. Pour batter into greased 16-cup plastic microwave fluted or straight-sided ring mold. Heat for 17 to 19 minutes, rotating dish 1/4 turn every 5 minutes. When done, top areas around center tube appear dry and set, but edges of cake appear moist and foamy. Let cake stand 10 minutes before inverting.

CRUMB CAKE

Approx. Cooking Time: 11 min.
Yield: 7 to 8 servings

1½ **cups sugar**
2 **cups sifted flour**
2 **teaspoons baking powder**
1½ **teaspoons cinnamon**
½ **cup softened butter or margarine**
2 **eggs, well beaten**
½ **cup milk**

1. Sift sugar, flour, baking powder and cinnamon together. Add butter and mix thoroughly. Set aside 1 cup of flour mixture for crumb topping.
2. Add eggs and milk. Blend well.
3. Pour batter into a lightly greased 8-inch round cake dish. Sprinkle the reserved crumb mixture on top and heat, uncovered, for 10 to 11 minutes giving dish ¼ turn every 3 minutes.

PECAN LOAF

Approx. Cooking Time: 7 min.
Yield: 3 to 4 servings

1 **cup sifted flour**
¾ **cup sugar**
¾ **teaspoon baking powder**
½ **teaspoon salt**
¼ **cup vegetable oil**
¼ **cup milk**
½ **teaspoon vanilla extract**
2 **egg whites**
¼ **cup coarsely chopped pecans**

1. Sift flour, sugar, baking powder and salt together into a medium mixing bowl.
2. Blend in oil, milk and vanilla. Beat with an electric mixer at medium speed for 2 minutes.
   Scrape sides and bottom of bowl several times.
3. Add egg whites and beat an additional 2 minutes, fold in nuts.
4. Pour batter into a lightly greased 8-inch square baking dish and heat, uncovered, for 5 to 7 minutes giving dish ¼ turn every 2 minutes.

CARROT SPICE CAKE

Approx. Cooking Time: 12 to 14 min.
Yield: 8 servings

1¼ **cups all-purpose flour**
1 **cup brown sugar**
1 **teaspoon baking powder**
1 **teaspoon baking soda**
1 **teaspoon ground cinnamon**
½ **teaspoon ground allspice**
½ **teaspoon salt**
1 **cup shredded carrots**
⅔ **cup oil**
2 **eggs**
½ **cup crushed pineapple with syrup**
1 **teaspoon vanilla extract**

1. Combine flour, sugar, baking powder, baking soda, cinnamon, allspice, salt and carrot. With electric mixer, stir in remaining ingredients and beat 2 minutes at medium speed.
2. Pour batter into greased 6-cup glass Bundt dish or 8-inch round baking dish with small glass inverted in center. Heat 12 to 14 minutes, giving dish ¼ turn every 4 minutes. Let stand, covered 10 minutes.
3. Store, covered, until ready to serve.

DEVIL'S FOOD CAKE

Approx. Cooking Time: 9 min.
Yield: 1 layer

¾ **cup sugar**
¼ **cup butter or margarine, softened**
1 **egg**
⅔ **cup hot water**
1 **cup all-purpose flour**
¼ **cup unsweetened cocoa**
¾ **teaspoon baking soda**
½ **teaspoon salt**
½ **teaspoon vanilla extract**

1. With electric mixer, cream sugar and butter; add egg and water. Stir in remaining ingredients and blend until smooth.
2. Into greased round 8-inch baking dish, pour batter. Heat 7 to 9 minutes, giving dish ¼ turn every 3 minutes. Let stand, covered 10 minutes.
3. Store, covered, until ready to serve.

CIDER SPICE CAKE

Approx. Cooking Time: 15 min.
Yield: 12 servings

2¼ **cups all-purpose flour**
  2 **teaspoons ground cinnamon**
  1 **teaspoon ground cloves**
  1 **teaspoon ground nutmeg**
  1 **teaspoon salt**
 ¾ **teaspoon baking soda**
1½ **cups sugar**
 ½ **cup butter or margarine, softened**
  1 **egg**
1¼ **cups apple cider or juice**
  1 **cup raisins**
  2 **tablespoons all-purpose flour**
    Confectioners sugar

1. Combine 2¼ cups flour, cinnamon, cloves, nutmeg, salt and baking soda. Set aside. With electric mixer, cream sugar and butter; add egg.
2. Alternately add flour mixture and cider, mixing until smooth; fold in raisins tossed with 2 tablespoons flour.
3. In greased 10 or 12-cup glass Bundt dish, pour batter; heat 13½ to 15 minutes, giving dish ¼ turn every 3 minutes.
4. Let stand, covered, 10 minutes, before inverting onto serving platter. Let stand, covered, until cool. Just before serving, sprinkle with confectioners sugar.

PLANTATION COCONUT CAKE

Approx. Cooking Time: 14 min.
Yield: 8 servings

  1 **package (18½ oz.) yellow cake mix**
  1 **package (3¾ oz.) instant coconut cream or toasted coconut pudding mix**
  4 **eggs**
  1 **cup water**
 ¼ **cup oil**
  1 **jar (12 oz.) strawberry or raspberry preserves**
    Creamy Glaze*
    Flaked coconut

1. With electric mixer, combine cake mix, pudding mix, eggs, water and oil; beat at medium speed 4 minutes.
2. In greased 10 to 12-cup glass Bundt dish, pour batter; heat 12 to 14 minutes, giving dish ¼ turn every 4 minutes. Let stand, covered, 15 minutes before inverting onto serving platter. Let stand, covered, until cool.
3. Split cake into 3 layers, spread in between each layer with preserves. Drizzle with Creamy Glaze and top with coconut. Store, covered, until ready to serve.

*Creamy Glaze: *Combine until smooth 1½ cups confectioners sugar, 2 to 2½ table-spoons milk and 2 tablespoons butter or margarine, softened. if desired, add 2 drops red food coloring.*

FESTIVE RUM CAKE

Approx. Cooking Time: 18 min.
Yield: 15 servings

  1 **cup finely chopped pecans or walnuts**
  1 **package (18½ oz.) yellow cake mix**
  1 **package (3¾ oz.) instant vanilla pudding mix**
  4 **eggs**
 ½ **cup water**
 ½ **cup oil**
 ½ **cup dark rum**
    *Rum Glaze

1. In generously greased 10 to 12-cup glass Bundt dish, sprinkle nuts. With electric mixer, combine cake mix, pudding mix, eggs, water, oil and rum; beat at medium speed 4 minutes. Pour batter evenly over nuts.
2. Heat 12 to 14 minutes, giving dish ¼ turn every 4 minutes. Let stand covered, 10 minutes. Prick top of cake; drizzle ½ Rum Glaze over cake.
3. Invert cake onto serving platter and prick top and sides of cake; drizzle cake with remaining glaze. Store, covered, until ready to serve.

*Rum Glaze

 ¼ **to ⅓ cup dark rum**
 ½ **cup butter or margarine**
  1 **cup sugar**
 ¼ **cup water**

1. In 2-cup glass measure, heat butter 1 to 1½ minutes until melted.
2. Stir in sugar and water and heat 3 to 3½ minutes until boiling; stir in rum.

SWEET-TART LEMON SQUARES

Approx. Cooking Time: 11 to 13 min.
Yield: 16 to 24 cookies

> 1 **can (14 oz.) sweetened condensed milk**
> 1/2 **cup lemon juice**
> 1 **teaspoon grated lemon rind (optional)**
> 1 1/2 **cups graham cracker crumbs**
> 1/2 **cup brown sugar**
> 1/2 **cup butter, melted**

1. In small mixing bowl stir together milk, lemon juice and rind, until thick and smooth. Set aside.
2. Mix together crumbs, sugar and butter. Place about 2/3 of mixture in 8-in square dish and press firmly into bottom of dish. Add milk mixture and spread evenly. Sprinkle remaining crumb mixture over top and pat down gently.
3. Heat 11 to 13 minutes giving dish 1/4 turn every 3 minutes. Cut in small squares as cookies or in larger pieces as dessert.

NUTTY CHIP CHEWS

Approx. Cooking Time: 10 to 12 min.
Yield: 10 to 12 bars

> 3/4 **cup brown sugar**
> 1/2 **cup butter or margarine, softened**
> 1 **egg**
> 1/4 **cup milk**
> 1 **teaspoon vanilla extract**
> 1/2 **teaspoon baking powder**
> 1 1/4 **cups all-purpose flour**
> 1/2 **cup chopped nuts**
> 1 **pkg. (6 oz.) semi-sweet chocolate pieces**

1. With electric mixer, cream sugar and butter; add egg, milk and vanilla. Stir in baking powder and flour until well blended; add nuts and 1/2 chocolate pieces.
2. Into greased 8-inch round baking dish, spread batter; top with remaining chocolate. Heat 10 to 12 minutes giving dish 1/4 turn every 3 minutes. Let stand, covered, until cool.

QUICK BAR COOKIES (FROM MIX)

Approx. Cooking Time: 7 min.
Yield: 16 bars

> 1 **package (12 oz.) chocolate chip cookie mix**

1. Prepare mix according to package direc-

tions. Spread dough into ungreased 8 or 9-inch round baking dish. Heat 5 to 7 minutes, giving dish 1/4 turn every 3 minutes.
2. Let stand, covered, until cool. Store, covered, until ready to serve.

QUICK RICE PUDDING

Approx. Cooking Time: 13 min.
Yield: 6 servings

> 3 **cups milk**
> 1/2 **cup packaged precooked rice**
> 1 **package (3 oz.) vanilla pudding and pie filling mix**
> 3 **tablespoon raisins***
> 1/4 **teaspoon ground cinnamon or nutmeg***

1. In 2-quart glass measure or bowl, combine all ingredients. Heat, covered with wax paper, 11 to 13 minutes until pudding is thickened, stirring three times. Chill before serving.

*Variatons: *Use 1 tablespoon orange liqueur and 1/4 cup chopped candied fruit for raisins and cinnamon.*

STEAMED DATE-NUT PUDDING

Approx. Cooking Time: 10 min.
Yield: 8 servings

> 1 1/4 **cups all-purpose flour**
> 1/2 **cup each chopped walnuts, dates and raisins**
> 1 **teaspoon ground cinnamon**
> 1/2 **teaspoon baking soda**
> 1/2 **teaspoon salt**
> 3/4 **cup hot water**
> 1/2 **cup molasses**
> 1 **egg**
> 2 **tablespoons butter or margarine, melted**

1. Combine flour, walnuts, dates, raisins, cinnamon, baking soda and salt; stir in water, molasses, egg and butter. Turn batter into greased 2-quart glass bowl with inverted glass in center.
2. Cover with plastic wrap. Heat 8 to 10 minutes giving dish 1/4 turn every 3 minutes. Let stand, covered, 10 minutes.
3. Invert onto serving platter; cover until cool. Serve with Vanilla Sauce, page 47.

STRAWBERRY SOUFFLE

Approx. Cooking Time: 6 min.
Yield: 6 to 8 servings

Water
2 packages (10 oz. ea.) frozen sliced strawberries in heavy syrup, thawed and drained (reserve syrup)
4 eggs, separated
2 envelopes unflavored gelatin
6 tablespoons sugar
6 drops red food coloring (optional)
1 cup (1/2 pt.) whipping or heavy cream, whipped

1. Add water to reserved syrup to equal 1 1/2 cups; stir in egg yolks. In large glass bowl, mix unflavored gelatin and 4 tablespoons sugar; stir in syrup mixture. Heat 5 to 6 minutes until gelatin is dissolved, stirring occasionally. Stir in food coloring and an additional 1 cup cold water.
2. Chill until mixture mounds slightly, stirring occasionally. Fold in strawberries. Beat egg whites until soft peaks form; gradually add remaining sugar and beat until stiff. Fold in gelatin mixture, then whipped cream. Turn into small souffle dish with 3-inch collar or 6 cup bowl; chill until firm.

GINGERBREAD PEAR COBBLER

Approx. Cooking Time: 13 min.
Yield: 6 servings

1 can (16 oz.) sliced pears, drained (reserve syrup)
1/2 cup raisins or chopped nuts
1 package (14 oz.) gingerbread mix
Water

1. Line bottom of 8-inch round baking dish with wax paper. Arrange pears on paper; top with raisins.
2. Prepare gingerbread according to package directions using reserved syrup as part of water.
3. Pour batter over pears. Heat 11 to 13 minutes, giving dish 1/4 turn every 3 minutes. Let stand, covered, until ready to serve.

RAISIN BREAD PUDDING

Approx. Cooking Time: 25 min.
Yield: 6 servings

2 cups milk
1/4 cup butter or margarine
5 eggs, beaten
1 cup sugar
1 teaspoon vanilla extract
4 cups cubed raisin bread (about 16 slices)
1/8 teaspoon ground cinnamon

1. In 1-quart glass measure, heat milk and butter 4 1/2 to 5 1/2 minutes until milk is scalded; quickly stir in eggs, 1/2 cup sugar and vanilla.
2. Meanwhile, in 3-quart casserole with inverted glass in center, arrange bread cubes; sprinkle with remaining sugar and cinnamon. Pour milk-egg mixture over bread. Heat covered, 17 to 19 minutes, giving dish 1/4 turn every 5 minutes, until pudding is set. Serve warm or chilled.

FRESH PEACH PIE

Approx. Cooking Time: 16 min.
Yield: 8 servings

2 pounds fresh peaches, peeled and sliced
1/2 cup brown sugar
1/2 tablespoon cornstarch
2 teaspoons lemon juice
1/2 teaspoon ground cinnamon (optional)
9-inch pastry shell, baked
Crumb Topping*

1. Toss peaches with sugar, cornstarch, lemon juice and cinnamon; arrange in prepared shell. Heat, covered, with wax paper, 6 to 9 minutes until peaches are almost tender.
2. Sprinkle with Crumb Topping; heat 6 to 7 1/2 minutes until topping is set. Let stand until cool.

*Crumb Topping: *Combine 1/2 cup all-purpose flour, 1/4 cup brown sugar, 1/4 cup butter or margarine, softened, 1/3 cup finely chopped nuts (optional) and 1/4 teaspoon ground cinnamon.*

FRUIT PIE

Approx. Cooking Time: 11 min.
Yield: 8 servings

- **1 can (21 oz.) favorite pie filling**
- **1/4 cup raisins (optional)**
- **1 teaspoon lemon or orange juice**
- **1/8 teaspoon ground cinnamon**
  8 or 9-inch pastry shell, baked
- **1/2 cup all-purpose flour**
- **1/4 cup brown sugar**
- **1/4 cup butter or margarine, softened**

1. Combine pie filling, raisins, lemon juice and cinnamon; pour into prepared crust.
2. Blend together remaining ingredients; crumble over filling. Heat 8 to 11 minutes until heated through; cool before serving.

DEEP DISH APPLE PIE

Approx. Cooking Time: 9 min.
Yield: 3 to 4 servings

- **2 1/2 cups apples, peeled and sliced**
- **1/4 cup sugar**
- **1 1/2 tablespoons water**
- **1/4 teaspoon cinnamon**
- **1/2 cup buttermilk biscuit mix**
- **1 tablespoon sugar**
- **1/4 cup milk**

1. Combine apples, 1/4 cup sugar, water and cinnamon in a deep, medium casserole dish. Stir thoroughly and heat for 2 to 3 1/2 minutes, covered.
2. While apples are cooking, combine biscuit mix, 1 tablespoon sugar and milk in a small mixing bowl. Stir with a fork until biscuit mix is moistened.
3. Drop biscuit batter onto hot apples by the spoonful. Cover and heat 3 1/2 to 5 minutes until topping is no longer doughy on the bottom side. Serve hot with a scoop of ice cream, if desired.

PECAN PIE

Approx. Cooking Time: 10 min.
Yield: 8 servings

- **1 cup dark corn syrup**
- **1/4 cup brown sugar**
- **3 eggs**
- **2 tablespoons butter or margarine, melted**
- **1 teaspoon vanilla extract**
- **3/4 cup chopped pecans**
  9-inch pastry shell, baked

1. Combine syrup, sugar, eggs, butter and vanilla; stir in pecans. Pour into prepared crust. Heat 8 to 10 minutes until pie is set.
2. Let stand until cool. Garnish, if desired, with sweetened whipped cream.

MAMA'S NUT PIE

Approx. Cooking Time: 10 to 11 min.
Yield: 8 servings

- **1 cup brown sugar**
- **1/2 cup sugar**
- **3 eggs**
- **1/2 cup evaporated milk**
- **1/2 cup chopped walnuts**
- **1 teaspoon vanilla extract**
- **1/8 teaspoon lemon extract**
  9-inch pastry shell, baked
  Sweetened whipped cream or whipped topping

1. Combine sugars, eggs, milk, walnuts, and extracts; pour into prepared shell. Heat 10 to 11 minutes giving dish 1/4 turn every 3 minutes until center is almost set.
2. Let stand, covered with wax paper, until cool. Just before serving, top with whipped cream.

GRASSHOPPER PIE

Approx. Cooking Time: 5 min.
Yield: 8 servings

- **3 cups miniature marshmallows**
- **1/2 cup milk**
- **3 tablespoons cream de cocoa**
- **3 tablespoons creme de menthe**
- **1 cup (1/2 pt.) whipping cream, whipped**
  9-inch chocolate cookie crumb crust, baked

1. In large glass bowl, heat marshmallows and milk 3 1/2 to 4 1/2 minutes; stir until smooth.
2. Stir in cream de cocoa and creme de menthe; chill until mixture mounds slightly. Fold in whipped cream and turn into prepared crust. Chill until firm.

CHOCOLATE ROCKY ROAD PIE

Approx. Cooking Time: 9 min.
Yield: 8 servings

- **1 package (3 5/8 oz.) chocolate pudding and pie filling mix**
- **1 3/4 cups milk**
- **1 to 1 1/2 cups miniature marshmallows**
- **1/2 to 1 cup coarsely chopped walnuts**
  9-inch chocolate cookie crumb crust, baked

1. In 4-cup glass measure, combine pudding mix and milk; heat 7 to 8 1/2 minutes until pudding is thickened, stirring twice.
2. Cool 5 minutes; fold in marshmallows and nuts. Turn into prepared crust; chill.

MARSHMALLOW CRISP

Approx. Cooking Time: 4 min.
Yield: 16 bars

- **1/4 cup butter**
- **20 marshmallows (half of 10 oz. package)**
- **2 1/2 cups crispy rice cereal**

1. Melt butter in 8-inch square baking dish about 1 minute.
2. Add marshmallows. Cover loosely with plastic wrap and heat for 3 minutes. Stir.
3. Add cereal. Blend and press firmly into dish.

PECAN PRALINES

Approx. Cooking Time: 13 min.
Yield: 1 1/2 dozen

- **1 cup brown sugar**
- **1 cup sugar**
- **1/3 cup light corn syrup**
- **1/4 cup water**
- **1 1/2 cups coarsely chopped pecans**
- **1 tablespoon butter or margarine**
- **1 teaspoon vanilla extract**

1. In medium glass bowl, combine sugars, corn syrup and water; heat 10 1/2 to 13 1/2 minutes until mixture reads 238°F (soft ball stage) when tested with candy thermometer*
2. Stir in pecans, butter and vanilla. Let stand 2 minutes. Drop by tablespoonfuls onto well greased wax paper lined cookie sheet; chill until set.

*Important: *Do not use candy thermometer in dish while operating the microwave oven.*

PEANUT BRITTLE

Approx. Cooking Time: 13 to 14 min.
Yield: 1 pound

- **1 cup sugar**
- **1/2 cup white corn syrup**
- **1 cup roasted, salted peanuts**
- **1 teaspoon butter**
- **1 teaspoon vanilla extract**
- **1 teaspoon baking soda**

1. In 1 1/2–qt. casserole, stir together sugar and syrup. Heat 5 to 6 minutes.
2. Stir in peanuts. Heat for 4 to 5 minutes, stirring after 2 1/2 minutes.
3. Add butter and vanilla to syrup, blending well. Heat for 2 to 3 minutes. Peanuts will be lightly browned and syrup very hot.
4. Add baking soda and stir gently until light and foamy. Pour mixture onto lightly buttered cookie sheet. Cool 1 hour. When cool, break into small pieces and store in air-tight container.

FAST FIXIN CHOCOLATE FUDGE

Approx. Cooking Time: 9 min.
Yield: 3 pounds

- **2 packages (16 oz. ea.)
  confectioners sugar**
- **1 cup unsweetened cocoa**
- **1/2 cup milk**
- **1 cup butter or margarine**
- **1 1/2 cups cups chopped nuts(optional)**
- **2 tablespoons vanilla extract**

1. In large bowl, mix sugar and cocoa. Add
   milk and butter (do not stir). Heat 6 1/2 to
   9 minutes until butter is melted; add nuts
   and vanilla, stirring until smooth.
2. Spread into well greased square baking
   dish; chill until firm. Cut into squares to
   serve.

Note: **For 1 1/2 pounds Fudge,** *follow
above procedure. Halve all ingredients, heat 3 to 4 1/2 minutes pour;
into greased loaf dish.*

Variation:
For ROCKY ROAD Fudge, *coarsely
chop nuts and add 1 cup miniature marshmallows.*

BUTTERSCOTCH FUDGE

Approx. Cooking Time: 16 min.
Yield: 3 pounds

- **3 cups sugar**
- **3/4 cup butter or margarine**
- **1 can (5 1/3 oz.) evaporated milk**
- **1 package (12 oz.) butterscotch
  flavored pieces***
- **1 jar (7 1/2 oz.) marshmallow creme**
- **1 cup chopped walnuts**
- **1 teaspoon vanilla extract**

1. In 2 1/2-quart casserole dish, combine
   sugar, butter and milk; heat 13 to 16
   minutes until sugar is dissolved, stirring
   twice.
2. Add remaining ingredients and stir until
   butterscotch is melted. Turn into well
   greased oblong baking dish. Chill until
   firm; cut into squares to serve.

*Variation:
For CHOCOLATE Fudge, *use 1 package
(12 oz.) semi-sweet chocolate pieces.*

TOFFEE FONDUE

Approx. Cooking Time: 6 min.
Yield: 6 servings

- **1 package (14 oz.) caramels**
- **1/4 cup strong coffee**
- **2 to 4 tablespoons milk**
- **1/2 cup milk chocolate pieces
  (optional)
  Dippers***

1. In medium glass bowl, combine caramels,
   coffee, milk and chocolate. Heat 5 to 6
   minutes, stirring twice until smooth.
2. Serve with assorted Dippers. If fondue
   gets cool, reheat 1 to 2 minutes.

*Dippers: *Apple and pear slices, banana
chunks, large marshmallows,
angel food or pound cake, cut
into 1 1/2-inch cubes.*

SWEET SPICED NUTS

Approx. Cooking Time: 7 to 8 min.
Yield: 1 1/2 cups

- **1/2 cup brown sugar**
- **1 1/2 tablespoons water**
- **1/2 teaspoon salt**
- **1/2 teaspoon ground cinnamon**
- **1/4 teaspoon ground allspice**
- **1/8 teaspoon ground cloves**
- **1/8 teaspoon ground nutmeg**
- **1 1/2 cups almonds, cashew, pecan
  halves or walnut halves or
  combination**

1. In 2-quart casserole dish, combine sugar
   water, salt, cinnamon, allspice, cloves
   and nutmeg. Heat 1 to 2 minutes until
   sugar is melted; stir in nuts.
2. Heat 5 to 6 1/2 minutes until syrup begins
   to harden. Spread nut mixture out on
   lightly buttered cookie sheet to cool.
3. Break into small pieces and store in
   airtight container.

BAKED GRAPEFRUIT

Approx. Cooking Time: 7 min.
Yield: 4 servings

> **2 medium grapefruits**
> **8 teaspoons brown sugar**
> **or maple syrup**
> **Ground cinnamon**

1. With sharp knife, cut each grapefruit in half; remove seeds and cut around each section.
2. On glass oven tray arrange grapefruit; sprinkle with brown sugar. Heat 5 to 6½ minutes; sprinkle with cinnamon before serving.

Note: For TWO servings, *follow above procedure. Halve all ingredients; heat 3 to 4½ minutes.*

BAKED APPLES

Approx. Cooking Time: 11 min.
Yield: 4 servings

> **4 medium baking apples (about 6 oz. ea.)**
> **¼ cup brown sugar**
> **2 tablespoons finely chopped nuts or raisins**
> **¼ teaspoon ground cinnamon**
> **2 tablespoons butter or margarine**
> **¼ cup water**

1. Core apples, leaving small plug in blossom end; peel skin 1-inch from top. Combine sugar, nuts and cinnamon; fill apples with mixture.
2. In baking dish, arrange apples; dot with butter and sprinkle with water. Heat, covered, 9 to 11 minutes, turning dish once. Let stand 7 minutes; serve warm or chilled, spooning sauce over apples.

Note: For TWO servings, *follow above procedure. Halve all ingredients; heat apples 4½ to 6 minutes.*
For ONE serving, *heat apple 2 to 3½ minutes.*

CURRIED FRUIT COMPOTE

Approx. Cooking Time: 16 min.
Yield: 6 servings

> **1 can (17 oz.) apricot halves, drained (reserve syrup)**
> **1 can (16 oz.) peach slices, drained (reserve syrup)**
> **¼ teaspoon curry powder**
> **¼ teaspoon ground cinnamon**
> **1 tablespoon cornstarch**
> **¼ cup water**
> **½ cup raisins**

1. In 2-cup glass measure, combine 1 cup reserved syrups, curry and cinnamon; heat 3 to 4½ minutes.
2. Stir in cornstarch blended with water and heat 2 to 3 minutes until slightly thickened, stirring occasionally.
3. In baking dish, combine apricots, peaches and raisins; heat 5 to 6½ minutes until heated through, stirring once.
4. Pour in sauce and heat 1½ to 2 minutes. Serve warm or chilled.

PEARS WITH CARAMEL SAUCE

Approx. Cooking Time: 18 min
Yield: 6 servings

> **6 large pears (6 oz. ea.)**
> **1 tablespoon sugar**
> **Dash ground cinnamon**
> **½ cup water**
> **30 caramels (about 10 oz.)**
> **2 tablespoons butter or margarine**
> **2 tablespoons rum (optional)**
> **1 tablespoon water**
> **½ teaspoon ground cinnamon**
> **Sweetened whipped cream**

1. Core pears and peel skin 1 inch from top. Combine sugar and dash cinnamon; sprinkle inside pears.
2. In oblong baking dish, arrange pears; sprinkle with ½ cup water. Heat, covered, 12 to 13½ minutes until pears are tender, turning dish once; cool or chill.
3. Just before serving, in glass bowl, combine caramels, butter, rum, 1 tablespoon water and ground cinnamon; heat 2 to 3 minutes, stirring twice until smooth.
4. Spoon sauce over pears; top with whipped cream.

CARAMEL APPLES

Approx. Cooking Time: 4 min.
Yield: 6 servings

- **1   package (14 oz.) caramels**
- **1   tablespoon hot water**
- **6   medium apples**
  Wooden ice cream sticks
  Finely chopped nuts

1. In 1½-quart casserole dish, heat caramels and water 3 to 4½ minutes until melted, stirring twice until smooth. Insert sticks into stem ends of apples.
2. Dip each apple into caramel mixture turning and tipping dish to coat apples; sprinkle with chopped nuts. Place on greased waxed paper lined cookie sheet; cool.

Hint: *If caramel mixture becomes too stiff while dipping apples, return to oven and heat ¾ to 1 minute.*

CHUNKY APPLE SAUCE

Approx. Cooking Time: 13 to 15 min.
Yield: 4 cups

- **3   pounds baking apples, peeled, cored and sliced (about 4 cups)**
- **¾   cup sugar to taste**
- **½   cup water**
- **½   to 1 teaspoon ground cinnamon**

1. In large glass bowl, combine all ingredients. Heat, covered with wax paper, 13 to 15 minutes until apples are soft, stirring once.
2. Mash apples until smooth; serve warm or chilled.

Note: For 2 cups applesauce, *follow above procedure. Halve all ingredients; heat apples 6 to 7 minutes.*

SPICY APPLES'N OATS

Approx. Cooking Time: 7 min.
Yield: 6 servings

- **4   large baking apples, peeled and sliced (about 1½ lbs.)**
- **⅔   cup brown sugar**
- **⅓   cup chopped nuts or raisins**
- **1   teaspoon ground cinnamon**

- **¼   teaspoon ground nutmeg**
- **⅓   cup butter or margarine, softened**
- **⅓   cup flour**
- **⅓   cup quick cooking oats**

1. In 8-inch round baking dish; layer ½ apples. Combine sugar, nuts, cinnamon and nutmeg; sprinkle ½ sugar mixture over apples.
2. Top with remaining apples. Into remaining sugar mixture, blend in butter, flour and oats; sprinkle over apples. Heat 6 to 7½ minutes giving dish ¼ turn every 3 minutes, until apples are tender.
   Let stand 7 minutes; serve warm or cool.

FRUIT COBBLER

Approx. Cooking Time: 16 min.
Yield: 6 servings

Filling:
- **2   cans (30 oz. ea.) peach slices or other canned fruit , drained (reserve ¼ cup syrup)**
- **3   tablespoons all-purpose flour**
- **½   tablespoon lemon juice**
- **½   tablespoon vanilla extract**
- **½   teaspoon ground cinnamon**

Topping:
- **1   cup buttermilk biscuit mix**
- **¼   cup brown sugar**
- **¼   cup butter or margarine, softened**
- **2   tablespoons hot water**

1. In square baking dish, combine Filling ingredients. Combine Topping ingredients, stirring until dough pulls away from sides of bowl and forms a ball.
2. Gently spread topping onto filling (topping will spread slightly when heated). Sprinkle, if desired, with additional cinnamon. Heat 13½ to 16½ minutes until topping is set. Let stand to cool.

*Variations:
For FRESH PEACH Cobbler, *combine 1½ pounds peeled and sliced peaches and ¼ to ⅓ cup brown sugar; heat, covered, 5 to 6 minutes until tender. Follow above procedure, omitting ¼ cup reserved liquid.*

For QUICK FRUIT Cobbler, *substitute 2 cans (21 oz. ea.) fruit pie filling and ¼ cup water for Filling ingredients.*

BREAKFAST FRUIT TART

Approx. Cooking Time: 8 min.
Yield: 4 servings

1½ **cups all-purpose flour***
½ **cup oil**
2 **tablespoons milk**
1 **tablespoon sugar**
1 **teaspoon salt**
⅓ **cup apricot, peach or favorite preserves**
Sliced fresh fruit or canned fruit, well drained

1. Combine flour, oil, milk, sugar and salt; pat onto bottom and sides of 9-inch glass pie plate. Prick with fork; heat 6½ to 8 minutes; cool.
2. In small glass bowl, heat preserves ½ minute or until melted. Arrange fruit on tart shell; drizzle with preserves. Cut into wedges to serve.

*Substitution: *Use ¾ cup whole wheat flour and ¾ cup all-purpose flour for 1½ cups all-purpose flour.*

BRANDIED PEACHES

Approx. Cooking Time: 6 min.
Yield: 4 servings

1 **can (29 oz.) peach halves, drained (reserve ½ cup syrup)**
⅔ **cup peach or pineapple preserves**
¼ **to ⅓ cup brandy**
1 **teaspoon lemon juice**
Toasted coconut

1. In baking dish, arrange peaches. Combine reserved syrup, preserves, brandy and lemon juice.
2. Pour over peaches; top with coconut. Heat, covered, 4½ to 6 minutes until heated through. Serve warm or chilled.

BUTTERSCOTCH BANANAS

Approx. Cooking Time: 5 to 7 min.
Yield: 4 servings

½ **cup brown sugar**
¼ **cup rum**
¼ **cup butter**
2 **large ripe, firm bananas**

1. In 1½-qt. casserole stir together brown sugar and rum. Add butter. Cover. Heat 4 to 5 minutes, stirring after 2 minutes, until sugar is dissolved.
2. Cut bananas lengthwise, then crosswise so there are 8 pieces. Add to syrup, stirring to coat each piece. Heat 1 to 2 minutes, until hot. Serve over ice cream.

MARBLE BROWNIES

Power Level: DEFROST
HIGH
Approx. Cooking Time: 14 min.
Yield: 40 brownies

1 **package (22½ to 23¾ oz.) fudge brownie mix**
2 **package (3 oz. ea.) cream cheese**
2 **tablespoons butter or margarine**
1 **egg**
¼ **cup sugar**
1 **tablespoon flour**
½ **teaspoon vanilla extract**

1. Prepare fudge-type brownies according to package directions. Spread 1 cup batter into each of 2 greased 8-inch round baking dishes.
2. In small glass bowl, heat cream cheese and butter 1½ minutes on DEFROST to soften; blend in remaining ingredients. Evenly divide cheese mixture into baking dishes; spoon remaining brownie batter on top. With knife, swirl gently to marble.
3. Heat one dish 10½ to 12½ minutes on HIGH giving dish ¼ turn every 3 minutes. Repeat procedure with remaining dish. Let stand, covered, until cool; store, covered, until ready to serve.

Pictured on the following page: Hot Buttered Rum, Irish Coffee, Apricot Tea ▶

CÂFE ROYALE

Approx. Cooking Time: 1½ min.
Yield: 6 demitasse servings

> **¼ to ½ cup brandy**
> **1 tablespoon sugar**
> **3 whole cloves**
> **1 stick cinnamon, broken**
> **Peel of 1 lemon or orange**
> **2 cups hot strong coffee**

1. In 1-cup glass measure, combine brandy, sugar, cloves, cinnamon and lemon peel. Heat 1 to 1½ minutes; stir.
2. Carefully flame and strain brandy into coffee. Serve in demitasse cups.

MULLED WINE

Approx. Cooking Time: 6 min.
Yield: 4 servings (6 oz. ea.)

> **3 cups Burgundy wine**
> **¼ cup brown sugar**
> **2 cinnamon sticks, broken**
> **Ground nutmeg**

1. In each of 4 mugs, combine ¾ cup wine, 1 tablespoon brown sugar, ½ cinnamon stick and dash nutmeg.
2. Heat 4½ to 6 minutes.

> **Note: For TWO servings,** *follow above procedure. Halve all ingredients; heat wine 3½ to 4½ minutes.*

IRISH COFFEE

Approx. Cooking Time: 5 min.
Yield: 4 servings (about 6 oz. ea.)

> **2 to 3 cups strong coffee**
> **4 teaspoons sugar**
> **6 ounces Irish whiskey**
> **Sweetened whipped cream**

1. Into each of 4 cups, pour ½ to ¾ cup coffee, heat 4 to 5 minutes.
2. For each drink, stir in 1 teaspoon sugar and 1½ ounces Irish whiskey; top with whipped cream.

> **Note: For TWO servings,** *follow above procedure. Halve all ingredients; heat coffee 2 to 3 minutes.*

HOT BUTTERED RUM

Approx. Cooking Time: 6 min.
Yield: 4 servings (about 6 oz. ea.)

> **2⅔ cups apple cider or water**
> **4 cinnamon sticks**
> **4 tablespoons brown sugar**
> **¾ cup rum**
> **4 teaspoons butter or margarine**
> **Ground nutmeg**

1. In each of 4 mugs, combine ⅔ cup cider, 1 cinnamon stick and 1 tablespoon sugar; heat 5 to 6 minutes.
2. For each drink, stir in approximately 1 tablespoon rum; top with 1 teaspoon butter and dash nutmeg.

> **Note: For TWO servings,** *follow above procedure. Halve all ingredients; heat cider 2 to 3 minutes.*

MULLED CIDER

Approx. Cooking Time: 5 min.
Yield: 2 servings

> **1½ cups apple juice or apple cider**
> **2 cinnamon sticks**
> **2 to 4 whole cloves (to taste)**
> **Nutmeg**
> **Whipped Cream**

1. Combine an equal amount of apple juice, whole cloves and cinnamon sticks in two mugs or cups.
2. Heat for 3½ to 5 minutes.
3. Do not allow apple juice to boil. Garnish with a dollop of whipped cream in each cup and sprinkle with nutmeg.

HOT MOCHA MILK

Approx. Cooking Time: 6 min.
Yield: 2 servings

- **3 tablespoons chocolate syrup**
- **1 teaspoon instant coffee**
- **1/4 teaspoon cinnamon**
- **1 1/2 cups milk**
  Whipped Cream

1. Combine an equal amount of chocolate syrup, instant coffee, and cinnamon in two mugs or cups.
2. Stir in milk: heat 4 to 6 minutes.
3. Do not allow milk to boil. Garnish with whipped cream.

WASSAIL CHEER

Power Level: HIGH
             DEFROST
Approx. Cooking Time: 19 min.
Yield: 6 servings (6 oz. ea.)

- **4 cups apple cider**
- **1/4 cup lemon juice**
- **1/4 cup brown sugar**
- **1/2 teaspoon whole allspice**
- **1/2 teaspoon whole cloves**
- **1/8 teaspoon ground nutmeg**

1. In medium glass bowl, combine all ingredients; heat 12 to 13 minutes on HIGH.
2. Continue cooking on DEFROST an additional 5 to 6 minutes. To serve, cool slightly; strain into mugs.

CRANAPPLE WARMER

Power Level: HIGH
             DEFROST
Approx. Cooking Time: 16 min.
Yield: 4 servings (6 oz. ea.)

- **3 cups cranapple or cranberry juice**
- **8 whole allspice**
- **8 whole cloves**
- **4 cinnamon sticks, broken**

1. In 4-cup glass measure, combine all ingredients; heat 7 to 9 minutes on HIGH.
2. Continue cooking on DEFROST an additional 7 minutes. To serve, cool slightly; strain into mugs.

APRICOT TEA

Approx. Cooking Time: 12 min.
Yield: 4 servings (8 oz. ea.)

- **3 cups water**
- **4 tea bags**
- **4 tablespoons apricot preserves**
- **4 tablespoons apricot brandy (optional)**
  Sugar to taste
  Sweetened whipped cream or whipped topping
  Ground nutmeg or cinnamon

1. Into each of 4 mugs, pour 3/4 cup water; heat 4 1/2 to 5 minutes.
2. For each drink, add one tea bag; brew 4 1/2 to 7 1/2 minutes. Stir in 1 tablespoon preserves, 1 tablespoon brandy and sugar.
3. Top with whipped cream and dash nutmeg.

Note: For TWO servings, *follow above procedure. Halve all ingredients; heat water 3 to 3 1/2 minutes.*

ORANGE BURST

Power Level: HIGH
             DEFROST
Approx. Cooking Time: 18 min.
Yield: 4 servings (8 oz. ea.)

- **3 cups apricot nectar**
- **1 cup orange juice**
- **2 cinnamon sticks, broken**
- **1 teaspoon whole cloves**

1. In 4-cup glass measure, combine all ingredients and heat 10 to 12 minutes on HIGH.
2. Continue cooking on DEFROST an additional 5 to 6 minutes. To serve, strain into mugs and garnish, if desired, with orange slices.

Memo

Pictured on the following page: Jam & Jelly, Liqueurs & Brandies, Dried Flowers ▶

Special Extras

JAM AND JELLY

With the help of your microwave oven, you can escape the toil associated with preparing these special sweets. Many of the jam basics will remain the same as you change to the microwave way. Just follow each recipe and the hints below to insure your first microwave jam will be the best ever.

- Use a large glass bowl or casserole dish.
- Stir mixture two or three times during first third of cooking to dissolve the sugar.
- Wait until the mixture comes to a full rolling boil as the recipes direct.
- Stir and skim foam off mixture, if necessary, (5 to 7 minutes).
- Ladle into hot sterilized glasses or jars. Seal with thin (1/8 to 1/4-inch) layer of **paraffin**.
- Properly sealed and stored (in a cool, dry place) jams and jellies will keep at least 1 year.

PEACH JAM

Approx. Cooking Time: 27 min.
Yield: 9 cups

- **4 cups sliced peeled, fresh peaches (about 3 lbs.)**
- **7 1/4 cups sugar**
- **1/4 cup lemon juice**
- **1/2 6-ounce bottle liquid pectin**

1. In large glass bowl, thoroughly combine peaches, sugar and lemon juice. Heat 22 to 26 minutes until mixture comes to a full boil, stirring occasionally during the first 5 minutes. Heat an additional 2 minutes.
2. Stir in pectin and skim off any foam. Ladle into glasses; seal with paraffin.

STRAWBERRY JAM

Approx. Cooking Time: 34 min.
Yield: 6 1/2 cups

- **4 packages (10 oz. ea.) frozen strawberries in heavy syrup, thawed**
- **5 cups sugar**
- **2 tablespoons lemon juice**
- **1/2 6-ounce bottle liquid pectin**

1. In large glass bowl, thoroughly combine strawberries, sugar and lemon juice. Heat 30 to 33 minutes until mixture comes to a full boil, stirring occasionally during first 10 minutes. Heat an additional 2 minutes.
2. Stir in pectin and skim off any foam. Ladle into glasses; seal with paraffin.

GRAPE JELLY

Approx. Cooking Time: 28 min.
Yield: 3 cups

- **2 cups grape juice**
- **3 1/2 cups sugar**
- **1/2 6-ounce bottle liquid pectin**

1. In large glass bowl, thoroughly combine juice and sugar. Heat 15 to 18 minutes until mixture is boiling, stirring twice during first 6 minutes of cooking.
2. Stir in pectin and heat 6 to 9 minutes until mixture comes to a full boil. Heat an additional 2 minutes skim off any foam.
3. Ladle into glasses; seal with paraffin.

Frozen Convenience Foods

ITEM	COOK TIME (in min.)	SPECIAL TECHNIQUES
APPETIZERS		
Bite Size	4 to 6	Arrange 12 to 15 appetizers at a time on paper towel lined plate or microwave oven roasting rack.
MAIN DISH		
Hearty T.V.-Style Dinner (17 oz.)	15 to 17	If container is 3/4-inch deep, remove foil cover and replace foil tray in original box.
Regular T.V.-Style Dinner (11 oz.)	7 to 10	
Entree		For containers more than 3/4-inch deep,
(8 to 9 oz.)	8 to 10	remove food to similar size glass container;
(21 oz.)	23 to 26	heat, covered. Stir occasionally.
(32 oz.)	26 to 28	if possible, or give container 1/4 turn after half of cooking time.
Macaroni and Cheese (8 oz.)	9 to 11	
Breakfast Entree (4 to 5 oz.)	3 to 4	
French Toast		
2 pieces	2 to 3	
4 pieces	3 to 4	
Waffles		
2 pieces	2 to 3	
4 pieces	3 to 4	
Fried Chicken		
2 pieces	5 to 7	Arrange on plate lined with 2 layers of paper towels.
4 pieces	8 to 9	
6 pieces	10 to 11	
Fried Fish Fillets		
2 fillets	4 to 5	
4 fillets	6 to 7	
Fish Cakes		
4 cakes	5 to 6	
Pizzas (individual)		
1	2 to 3	Arrange on microwave oven roasting rack.
2	4 to 5	
4	7 to 8	
Pouch Dinners		
(5 to 6 oz.)	5 to 7	Pierce pouch, set on saucer.
(10 to 11 oz.)	10 to 11	
SIDE DISHES		
Baked Stuffed Potatoes		
2	8 to 10	Arrange on plate. Let stand 5 minutes after cooking
4	12 to 14	
Vegetables in Pouches	11 to 13	Pierce pouch, set on saucer.
Frozen Potato Puffs (10 oz.)	4 to 6	Heat on plate, lined with paper towel.

*For best results, give foods 1/4 turn after half of total cooking time.

COOKING CANNED GOODS

- Empty contents of can into serving dish.
- Heat, covered.
- Stir after half of cooking time.
- After cooking, let stand 5 minutes before serving.

ITEM	COOK TIME (in min.)
Baked Beans (8 oz.)	3 to 4
(15 to 16 oz.)	6 to 7
Chow Mein (15 to 16 oz.)	7 to 8
Corned Beef Hash (15 oz.)	6 to 7
Macaroni and Cheese (15 oz.)	7 to 8
Sloppy Joe (15 oz.)	6 to 7
Ravioli (15 oz.)	7 to 8

Ingredient Substitution

The following is a list of foods and acceptable substitutes for emergencies:

Baking powder (1 t.) ········ 1/4 teaspoon baking soda *plus* 1/2 teaspoon cream of tartar

Buttermilk (1 cup) ········ 1 cup milk *plus* 1 tablespoon vinegar OR lemon juice

Chocolate, Semi-Sweet (2 oz.) ······ 1/3 cup semi-sweet chocolate pieces

Chocolate, Unsweetened (1 oz.) ······ 3 tablespoons cocoa *plus 1* tablespoon shortening

Corn Syrup (1/2 cup) ······ 1/2 cup sugar plus 2 tablespoons liquid

Cornstarch (1 t.) ········ 2 tablespoons flour

Cake Flour (1 cup) ········ 3/4 cup and 2 tablespoons all-purpose flour *plus* 2 tablespoons cornstarch

Garlic (1 clove) ·········· 1/8 teaspoon dried garlic flakes OR garlic powder

Grated Fresh Fruit Peel (1 T.) ·············· 1/2 teaspoon dried grated peel

Green Pepper (2 T. chopped) ·········· 1 tablespoon dried pepper flakes

Herbs, Fresh (1 t.) ········ 1/3 to 1/2 teaspoon dried

Honey (1 cup) ·········· 1 1/4 cups sugar *plus* 1/4 cup liquid

Milk (1 cup) ·········· 1/2 cup evaporated milk *plus* 1/2 cup water OR 1/4 cup non fat dry milk powder *plus* 1 cup water and 2 tablespoons butter

Onion (1/4 cup chopped) ········ 1 tablespoon dried onion flakes OR 1 teaspoon onion powder

Defrosting Guide

FOOD	AMOUNT	FIRST HALF TIME/ MINUTES	SECOND HALF TIME/ MINUTES	COMMENTS
MEAT				
Bacon	1 package	2 to 3 per lb.	2 to 3 per lb.	Place unopened package in microwave oven. Turn over after first ½ of time. Let stand 5 minutes. Microwave just until strips can be separated.
Franks	1 pound ½ pound	3 to 5 1½ to 2½	None None	Place unopened package in microwave oven. Microwave just until franks can be separated.
Ground, Beef & Pork	1 pound	3	3	Scrape off softened meat after second ½ of time. Set aside. Break up remaining block, microwave 2 to 3 minutes more.
	2 pounds	4	3½ to 4	Turn end to end after first ½ of time. Scrape off softened meat after second ½ of time. Set aside. Break up remaining block, microwave 1 to 2 minutes more.
Spareribs, Pork (2 lbs.)	1 package	2 to 4 per lb.	2 to 3 per lb.	Place wrapped package in microwave oven. Turn over after first ½ of time. After second ½ of time separate pieces with table knife. Let stand to complete defrosting.
Steaks, Chops & Cutlets; Beef, Lamb, Pork & Veal	1 package	2 to 4 per lb.	2 to 4 per lb.	Place wrapped package in microwave oven. Turn over after first ½ of time. After second ½ of time, separate pieces with table knife, let stand to complete defrosting.
Sausage, Bulk	1-lb. tray or roll	2 to 3	2 to 3	Scrape off softened meat after second ½ of time. Set aside. Break up remaining block, microwave 2 to 3 minutes more. Turn roll over after first ½ of time.
Sausage, Link	1 pound	2	1 to 2	Turn over after first ½ of time.
Sausage, Patties	12-oz. pkg.	2	1 to 2	Turn over after first ½ of time. Let stand 5 minutes.
POULTRY				
Chicken, Broiler-fryer, Cut up	2½ to 3 1b.	7 to 8	7 to 8	Place wrapped chicken in microwave oven. After ½ of time, unwrap and turn over. After second ½ of time, separate pieces and place in cooking dish. Microwave 2 to 4 minutes more, if necessary.
Whole	2½ to 3 lb.	9 to 11	9 to 11	Place wrapped chicken in microwave oven. After ½ of time, shield warm areas with foil.

Defrosting Guide

FOOD	AMOUNT	FIRST HALF TIME/ MINUTES	SECOND HALF TIME/ MINUTES	COMMENTS
FISH & SEAFOOD				
Fillets	1 pound	4	4 to 6	Place unopened package in microwave oven. (If fish is frozen in water, place in cooking dish.) Rotate ¼ turn after first ½ of time. After second ½ of time, hold under cold water to separate.
Shellfish, small pieces	1 pound	3½ to 4	3½ to 4	Spread shellfish in single layer in baking dish. Rearrange pieces after first ½ of time.
Shellfish, blocks Crab Meat	6-oz. pkg.	2 to 3	2 to 3	Place block in casserole. Turn over and break up with fork after first ½ of time.
Shellfish, large Crab Legs	1 to 2 8 to 10-oz.	3	2½ to 3	Arrange in cooking dish with light underside up. Turn over after first ½ of time.
BREADS, CAKES				
Bread or Buns	1-lb. pkg.	1	1½ to 2	Turn over after first ½ of time.
Heat & Serve Rolls	7-oz. pkg.	1	½ to 1	Rotate ½ turn after first ½ of time.
Coffee Cake	9 to 13-oz.	1	1½ to 2	Rotate ½ turn after first ½ of time.
Sweet Rolls	8¾ to 12-oz.	2	1½ to 2½	Rotate ½ turn after first ½ of time.
Doughnuts	1 to 3	½ to 1	None	No turn needed.
Doughnuts, Glazed	1 box of 12	2	2 to 3	Rotate ½ turn after first ½ of time.
French Toast	2 slices	2	1½ to 2	Rotate ½ turn after first ½ of time.
Cake, frosted	2 to 3 layer 17-oz.	1	1 to 2	Rotate ½ turn after first ½ of time.
Pound Cake	11 ¼-oz.	1 to 2	1 to 2	Rotate ½ turn after first ½ of time.
Cheesecake, plain or fruit top	17 to 19-oz.	2	2 to 3	Rotate ¼ turn after first ½ of time. Let stand 5 minutes to complete defrosting.
Fruit	10 to 16-oz.	1¼	1¼	Remove foil. Place package in microwave oven. After first ½ of time, break up with fork. Repeat if necessary.
Fruit, plastic pouch	1 to 2 10-oz. pkgs.	2	1 to 2	Place package in microwave oven. After first timing, flex package.
Fruit or Nut Pie	1 8-in.	3½ to 4	3 to 5	Rotate ½ turn after first timing.
Cream or Custard Pie	1 14-oz.	1 ½	1 to 2½	Rotate ½ turn after first ½ of time.

Index

Printed in Korea